TAKING SCIENCE TO THE EXTREME!

YOUNG SCIENTIST CHALLENGE

Discovery CHANNEL

By Rosanna Hansen and Sherry Gerstein
Foreword by Steven Jacobs

Discovery CHANNEL®

JB JOSSEY-BASS
A Wiley Imprint
www.josseybass.com

Discovery Communications would like to thank the following **Discovery Channel Young Scientist Challenge** judges for hard work and dedication to science:

Timothy Gatschet, RayAnn Havasy, Judith Heberling, Richard Hudson, Michael Husband, Hector Ibarra, Steven Jacobs, Anne Jefferson, Jennifer Kottler, Mark Oleksak, Blair Potter, Robert Starr, Linda Stevens, John Sutton, William White

The authors would like to thank Katherine Silkin and Michele Glidden of Science Service and Dr. Corwith Hansen of Scarsdale Public Schools, who provided valuable help and information during the research and writing of this book.

Published by Jossey-Bass
A Wiley Imprint
989 Market Street, San Francisco, CA 94103-1741
www.josseybass.com

Developed by Nancy Hall, Inc.
Designed by Iram Khandwala
Cover design by Chris Wallace

Discovery Channel Young Scientist Challenge: Taking Science to the Extreme! Book Development Team
Jane Root, General Manager, Discovery Channel
Gena McCarthy, Executive Producer, Discovery Channel
Carol LeBlanc, Vice President, Licensing
Elizabeth Bakacs, Vice President, Creative Services
Caitlin Erb, Marketing Associate

Library of Congress Cataloging-in-Publication Data

Hansen, Rosanna, and Gerstein, Sherry
  Discovery Channel young scientist challenge : taking science to the extreme! / Rosanna Hansen and Sherry Gerstein.
    p. cm.
  Includes index.
  ISBN 0-7879-8493-0 (pbk.)
1. Science—Experiments. 2. Science projects. I. Discovery Channel (Firm) II. Title.
  Q182.3.H36 2006
  507.8—dc22   2006012334

Printed in China
first edition

10 9 8 7 6 5 4 3 2 1

FOREWORD

*N*early 200 years ago, the teenage son of a poor blacksmith read a book he was repairing in a bookbinder's shop: Jane Marcet's *Conversations on Chemistry*. This book captured the imagination of the young man, Michael Faraday. From then on, he delighted in learning of recent discoveries in the fledgling field of science. That interest led him to a position at the Royal Institution of Great Britain, where Faraday made many great scientific discoveries of his own. However, he is most renowned for his ability to communicate science to the public.

Imagine the apprehension people of that time may have felt regarding the fiery sparks of a new discovery called "electricity." Faraday's ability to use common language to explain the nature of the unnerving electrical current soothed his audience and also engaged them in the delight of many profound scientific discoveries. Michael Faraday was indeed a masterful science communicator.

Since then, other science communicators have answered the call to provide common sense and understanding of scientific innovations. At the end of World War II, the first atomic bomb left most of the public fearful of anything tagged "nuclear." Dr. Hubert Alyea at Princeton University was engaged by the United Nations to visit 88 countries and explain the nature and positive possibilities of atomic energy to millions in attentive audiences.

In the 1950s, when the Sputnik satellite began the space race and subsequent pursuit of science learning, the public turned to yet another renowned science communicator. For several decades, youngsters were inspired to learn the "science of everyday living" from Don Herbert, better known as television's Mr. Wizard.

I was fortunate enough to be mentored by two of those famed science communicators. Alyea taught me chemistry and the art of being a scientific storyteller. Mr. Wizard trained me to follow in his footsteps in television.

My career as a science communicator has been a delightful adventure. However, as my retirement approaches, I realize the necessity for finding and mentoring the next generation of young science communicators. The world's current reliance on technology and scientific discovery has created, more than ever, a need for access to sound information presented by a fluent and sympathetic scientist.

To my delight, an unprecedented bit of corporate wisdom and generosity was afforded us all when Discovery Communications elected to create the **Discovery Channel Young Scientist Challenge**. The **DCYSC** has not only become the most prestigious science competition for America's middle school students, but also provided a method for identifying and supporting talented young science communicators at the dawn of their careers.

I have been head judge of the competition since its inception, and I am glad to report that I have seen some young Michael Faradays in our midst. This book explains, in part, how the **DCYSC** discovers and honors those girls and boys who are proficient in the skills of science and worthy of the title Young Science Communicator.

Steven Jacobs
Head Judge
Discovery Channel Young Scientist Challenge

CONTENTS

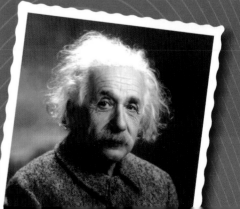

INTRODUCTION

Every October, 40 of America's brightest middle school scientists gather in Washington, D.C. They've come to compete in the **Discovery Channel Young Scientist Challenge (DCYSC)** for the title of America's Top Young Scientist of the Year—not to mention more than $100,000 in scholarships and other prizes.

The **Discovery Channel Young Scientist Challenge** is the only science contest of its kind for students in grades five through eight. The judges look for individuals who are more than top science students. They also have to be good science communicators, who can make science fun and understandable to others and inspire future generations of scientists.

The competition starts when more than 60,000 middle graders enter a science project in one of the science and engineering fairs affiliated with Science Service. Of these participants, 6,000 are nominated by the science fair directors to enter their projects in the **Discovery Channel Young Scientist Challenge**.

Between June and September, the **DCYSC** judges sift through the applications of the nominees to choose 400 semifinalists. The students are judged on the soundness of their work in addition to how well they can explain their ideas to others. In other words, communication is key.

The judges then pick 40 finalists who receive a weeklong, all-expense-paid trip to Washington, D.C., for the competition finals. There, they first present their individual science projects to the judges. Next, the students are assigned to teams that will take part in several thematically related challenges—all developed by Steven Jacobs, the head judge. In 2003, the **DCYSC** theme celebrated 100 years of aviation history, starting with the Wright brothers' first flight. The next year, 2004, commemorated the nearly 100 years since Albert Einstein published his special theory of relativity and made several other important discoveries. And the 2005 **DCYSC**, during the year that saw the south Asian tsunami and hurricanes Rita and Katrina, paid homage to the most ferocious forces of nature.

Science Process Skills

While the DCYSC judges watched the teams move through the challenges, one of the things they looked for was a team's use of science process skills, including:

- Measuring
- Comparing
- Analyzing
- Predicting
- Use of data collection equipment
- Problem solving
- Modeling
- Safety

At the end of the **DCYSC** week, one team is awarded a special dream trip. Then comes the moment everyone has been waiting for: the announcement of the first-, second-, and third-place individual winners. About 30 percent of an individual's score is based on his or her science project presentation. The remaining 70 percent is based on an individual's participation in the team challenges. Participants are evaluated for communication and leadership skills as well as for problem solving and other science process skills.

All finalists receive a $500 scholarship. The third place winner receives a $5,000 scholarship, the second place winner a $10,000 scholarship, and the first place winner takes home $20,000 in scholarship money—and the title of Discovery Channel's Top Young Scientist of the Year. Additional prizes—a session at Space Camp or a chance to go on an archaeological dig, for instance—are awarded to finalists who demonstrate special skills and talents during the competition. And to add to the fun, highlights of the **DCYSC** are broadcast on Discovery Channel for everyone in America to enjoy!

Ready to apply? You can find out how to enter on page 92. But first, turn the page to begin reading about what the **DCYSC** was like for the 40 finalists in 2003, 2004, and 2005. Then take a look at the Idea Files, which describe 40 of the winning science projects, for inspiration. To put it all together, check out the Science Project Handbook. ***Discovery Channel Young Scientist Challenge:*** *Taking Science to the Extreme!* is all you need to get started on your way to mastering your own science challenge! Good luck!

1 Forces of NATURE

When the forces of nature go extreme, watch out! That's when tornadoes, tsunamis, hurricanes, or earthquakes can happen. Scientists need to understand these awesome natural events, so that they can predict when and where they will happen in time to warn people. They can also help figure out ways to make structures that can better withstand powerful natural forces.

Tsunami damage

Tornado

Hurricane

It's Only Natural!

Earthquakes, volcanic eruptions, and tsunamis happen when tectonic plates—the large pieces of Earth's crust that "float" above the molten rock of the mantle—suddenly jerk apart, crash together, or grind up against each other. Extreme examples of plate movements are responsible for building mountain ranges, such as the Himalayas in southeast Asia, and forming major depressions, like the Great Rift Valley in eastern Africa.

Weather results from a combination of sunlight, the water cycle, and moving masses of air. When air warmed by the sun rises, cold air sweeps in to take its place. These movements in the atmosphere create winds, which are also affected by Earth's rotation. As the sun warms the oceans, water evaporates and vapor rises into the air, eventually forming clouds and falling back to Earth as rain, hail, sleet, or snow. When conditions are just right, severe weather can result in blizzards, ice storms, heavy fog, and the hurricanes and powerful thunderstorms that produce tornadoes.

For this competition, the finalists were divided into eight teams. Then they met with the judges and their host, J. D. Roth, the producer of *Endurance* on **Discovery KIDS**. For the challenges, each team would recreate three natural forces: a tsunami, a tornado, and a deadly fog bank. Finally, the teams would dispose of the dangerous fallout from a natural disaster and test their science skills in two bonus challenges. The teams would have just 90 minutes to complete each challenge.

Eye on the Storm

Challenge 1

Tornadoes are among the most destructive forces in nature. With wind speeds of up to 300 miles per hour, a tornado can lay waste to everything in its path, killing people and animals, destroying millions of dollars worth of property, and flattening entire towns and villages. Most of the violent tornadoes in the world occur near the center of the United States in an area called Tornado Alley, where several hundred tornadoes a year sweep across the land. For hands-on learning, the judges created a tornado challenge—and told the kids to give it a whirl!

Judge Mark Oleksak, president of Showboard, a science fair resource company, explained their assignment: Create a vortex (a whirling mass of air or water) by positioning several smaller fans below a huge ceiling fan so that the rising column of air starts to spin. Then measure the air pressure (barometric pressure) and wind speed both inside and outside the vortex—without disturbing the whirling winds. Their last task was to compare their measurements to their prediction, or hypothesis. Sounds simple, right? Not exactly—and the teams had only 90 minutes to get it right.

Fantastic!

First, the teams looked over their equipment. Positioned high above them was a huge cyclone fan 15 feet in diameter. When this fan switched on, it sucked up a column of air at 33,000 cubic feet per minute—enough to suck all the air from an average-size bedroom in just one second! Below the cyclone fan, smaller fans were positioned around the edge of a platform. In the middle of the platform, smoke-filled air billowed through a hole. The smoke would help them see the movement of the air. Nearby was a table with computers, weather instruments that measured air pressure and wind speed, and other apparatus.

I'm taking this home!

I hope this works!

Spinning into High Gear

To make a vortex, each team had to figure out exactly how to position the smaller fans around the platform. Team Gray set to work by analyzing the problem. They noticed that the platform fans blew the air in straight lines. Somehow, the team needed to position those fans correctly to create the circular air motion of a tornado. After brainstorming, they came up with a plan. The team carefully taped lines on the platform, using intersecting straight lines to create a circle. Then they lined up the platform fans with the taped lines. Great work so far, but with only 40 minutes left, Team Gray was still positioning their fans. They needed to spin into high gear!

Out of the Blue

While Team Gray worked methodically, Team Blue took a totally different approach. Using trial and error, they guessed what might be the right position for the fans. By chance, they happened to move the fans to the right place. That bit of luck meant Team Blue created the first vortex.

We did it!

Under Pressure

Now the pressure was on. Could Team Gray catch up? With 40 minutes to go, they made their first try to create a vortex—and failed. After repositioning the fans, they tried again. "Stop the fans!" shouted Anudeep Gosal. "The vortex is too narrow," he explained to his teammates. "We need to open the angle of the fans to make the vortex bigger and stronger." The team agreed, reset the fans—and *whoosh!* A giant vortex swirled up, 30 feet high. Team Gray's teamwork and Anudeep's leadership had paid off.

Weather Forecast

Next, Team Gray pooled their ideas to predict the result. "Our prediction is that the air pressure will go down inside the vortex," said Elijah Mena.

"And the wind speed will be higher inside it than outside," said another teammate.

Team Gray decided to use a barometer to measure the air pressure and an anemometer to measure the wind speed. Luckily, the equipment included a measuring device with both these instruments. Now, they had to figure out how to place the measuring device inside a vortex without blocking its winds. The team quickly came up with a good solution: Fasten the device to a long stick and push it all the way into the vortex from the outside.

Now listen up.

Measuring Up

Finally, Team Gray turned the fans back on, and another huge vortex swirled up to the ceiling. Colleen Ryan crawled along the platform and pushed the stick with the measuring device into the center of the vortex. After Colleen had taken the measurements, everyone gathered around to analyze the data. Sure enough, the barometric (air pressure) reading was lower inside the vortex than outside—and the wind speed was over 35 miles per hour. Outside the vortex, they found that the opposite was true: The air pressure was higher, and the wind speed was much lower.

A judge demonstrates the Bernoulli principle.

Bernoulli Principle

In 1738, the Swiss mathematician Daniel Bernoulli observed that water or air moving through a pipe went faster when the size of the pipe was reduced. Something was making the water or air move faster—but what? Bernoulli reasoned that the faster any fluid (liquid or gas) moved, the more its pressure dropped. Likewise, the slower the fluid, the more its pressure would rise. Today, we call his discovery the Bernoulli principle. Here's the way you might find his principle stated in a physics book: When the speed of a moving fluid (such as air or water) increases, the pressure within the fluid decreases.

A tornado vortex is one example of the Bernoulli principle at work. When a tornado forms, its winds start to spin faster and faster. The faster they swirl, the more the air pressure inside the vortex drops. The lower the air pressure, the faster the winds spin. Many tornadoes have winds of over 50 miles per hour, and some even reach speeds of 300 miles per hour.

Whirlwind Finish

High fives all around! Team Gray had predicted the correct results, using teamwork, good communication skills, and scientific problem solving. Their reward: first place in the Tornado Challenge. Second place went to Team Blue, with Team Orange placing third.

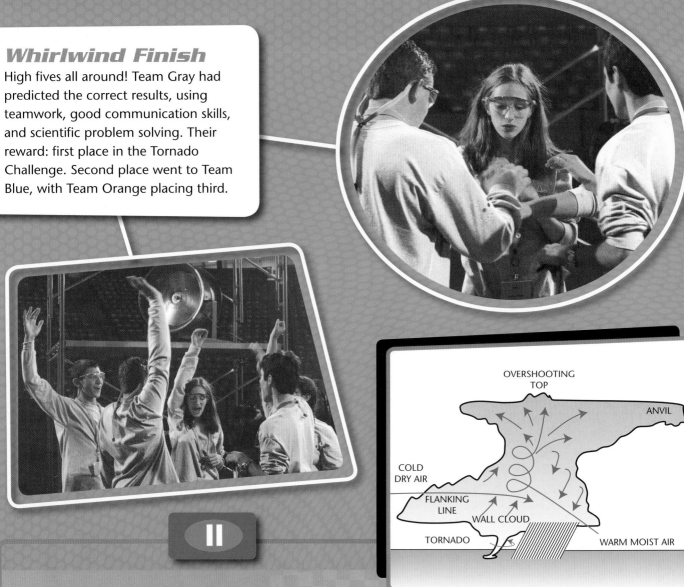

Into the Whirlwind

Tornadoes most often form in powerful thunderstorms called supercells. Thunderstorms start when warm, moist air moves in below cold, dry air. The warm air rises up and cools quickly, letting go of heat and water. More air rushes in from all sides, taking the place of the rising warm air and causing a powerful updraft. When there's also a strong vertical wind shear (wind that changes speed and direction with height), the thunderstorm's updraft causes it to rotate. At the same time, the rapidly rising air causes a sharp decrease in the air pressure. Low air pressure means increased wind speed. The rapidly spinning air decreases the air pressure even further, feeding the updraft.

As the air inside the storm spins faster and faster, vortexes may form inside and probably near the bottom of the rotating thunderclouds. These vortexes can turn into funnel clouds that extend down from the clouds. When they reach the ground, the funnel clouds are called tornadoes.

A tsunami is a series of ocean waves usually set in motion by an earthquake. The sudden movement of the ocean floor displaces, or moves, the overlying water, creating a series of waves. In deep water, tsunami waves move hundreds of miles per hour, are spaced tens of miles apart, and are only a few feet high. It's not until these waves reach a coastline and the ocean floor becomes shallower that the waves begin to slow down and pile up. This is when they can become a towering wall of water that hits the shore and races inland, snapping trees, smashing buildings, and destroying everything in its path.

It's important for scientists to understand and try to predict dangerous tsunamis, so the **DCYSC** judges created a tsunami challenge for hands-on learning. For this challenge, the teams confronted a wave tank 40 feet long and half full of water. Next to the tank was a table filled with wooden boards, sheet metal, plastic slabs, saws, hammers, and other tools.

As the team members looked over the tsunami set-up, judges Bill White and Anne Jefferson told them their assignment: Build a wave maker at one end of the 40-foot tank that can send powerful, consistent waves its entire length. At the other end, design and test various beach slopes and predict which ones are more prone to tsunami damage. Finally, prepare a short video report on the project.

Divide and Conquer

Team Blue split into two groups, with one group working on model beach slopes while the other group built the wave maker. Mary Lou Hedberg quickly came up with a design for the wave maker and showed her group how to build it. She took a long board, screwed bolts on both sides, added side boards and a backstop, and mounted it over the wave tank. With her design, the board acted like a lever, the bolts formed a pivot point, and the backstop kept the wave action consistent. Time after time, Team Blue's waves rolled past the same high point marked on the side of the tank.

Starting at the Bottom

Team Gold took a completely different approach with their wave maker. They focused on the fact that tsunami waves are generated from the ocean floor, unlike normal wind-generated waves. They built a wave maker with a block of wood at the end to push water starting from the very bottom of the tank.

Hitting the Beach

Once their wave maker was ready, Nilesh Tripuraneni led Team Gold in figuring out the slope of their beach. Nilesh reasoned that hitting a short, steep beach slope would push the wave higher, but it would break suddenly, losing its energy. When the wave hit a long, shallow beach slope, however, the wave would be lower but roll farther inland. Nilesh's teammates agreed with his reasoning, and they hurried to build their model beach slope.

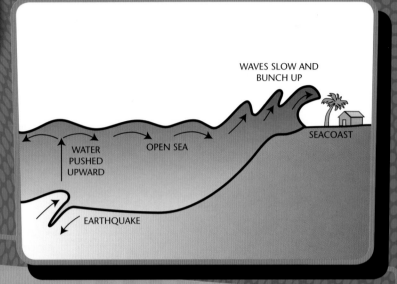

WAVES SLOW AND BUNCH UP

WATER PUSHED UPWARD

OPEN SEA

SEACOAST

EARTHQUAKE

Disturbance in the Deep

Tsunami waves are created when the bottom of the ocean moves suddenly, most often because of an earthquake, but sometimes because of a landslide, volcanic eruption, meteor impact, or explosion. These waves are unlike other waves in that they extend all the way from the seafloor to the water's surface and can be more than 100 miles long in open sea. In very deep water, tsunami waves can travel at more than 500 miles per hour. At the same time, the height of the wave crests may be only a few feet above the ocean's surface. Because of this, tsunami waves can pass under a ship in deep water without being noticed or identified.

As the ocean gets shallower near a coastline, the space between tsunami waves shortens and the waves begin to slow down. This causes an increase in the height of the waves. As the ocean floor continues to rise, the lower parts of the waves encounter more resistance and continue to lose speed. The upper parts of the waves, however, keep moving at the same speed, carrying the wave crests forward more rapidly. When there is not enough water underneath the crests to support them, the waves break.

On coastlines with steep beach slopes, tsunami waves break close to the shore, but their energy is concentrated in a small area and much of their power is reflected back out to sea. On gradual beach slopes, waves break farther from the shore but then bunch up into a wall of water moving forward. This means that in places with gradual slopes and low land, tsunami waves can rush farther inland.

Making Waves

Team Red used yet another approach for making waves. They took a long board and pushed it through the water like a paddle, without adding bolts or a backstop to control it. Their simple paddle sent wave after giant wave splashing down the tank. But soon they hit a snag—they didn't know what to do next.

Judgment Call

Judge Bill White came over to help Team Red members analyze their work. "To generate consistent waves, you must eliminate variables from the wave maker," he said. "Are you guys pushing the same amount of water every time?"

With that, Team Red realized that their simple wave maker couldn't make consistent and repeatable waves. "We need a better wave maker, fast!" said Taylor Jones.

Surging Ahead

With 45 minutes to go, Team Blue focused on the end of the wave tank where Neela Thangada and her group had built an artificial beach out of boards and plastic. With Mary Lou's wave maker sending consistent waves rolling her way, Neela could measure the height of the waves when they hit the beach. The splash height of each wave represented the power of a tsunami wave.

Recording Session

With time to spare, Team Blue put together a videotape that showed their wave maker in action and explained their project.

"Making the video is just as important as performing the experiment," said head judge Steven Jacobs. "Scientists need strong communication skills to get across their ideas and information."

Reaching Shore

When all the teams were finished, the judges added up the scores. Team Blue's excellent wave maker, scientific method, and communication skills had paid off. Blue swept into first place for the Tsunami Science challenge. Second place went to Team Gray, with Team Gold a close third.

Quick! Control That Variable!

When scientists do experiments, some parts of the experiment are always kept the same while other parts can change. Any part of an experiment that can change is called a variable. Each time scientists repeat an experiment, they need to measure how a variable has changed.

In the tsunami experiment, the length of the tank and the amount of the water in the tank were constants: They did not change. The volume of water pushed by the wave maker and the slope of the artificial beach could both change, so they were variables.

Here's the tricky part: Only one variable can be changed at a time. To study different slopes on the beach, the teams had to keep their waves consistent. That way, only the beach slope variable would change, and they could draw conclusions about that variable. If more than one variable were changed, the experimenters wouldn't know which variable produced a particular effect.

Waves of Destruction

Tsunamis can threaten the lives and homes of anyone who lives near the ocean. Here are three of the most destructive tsunamis in history and the event that caused each one:

When a huge volcanic explosion blew apart the small Indonesian island of Krakatau in August 1883, the boom from its blast was heard more than 2,170 miles away. Clouds of dust and ash rose up to 50 miles into the air and were carried around the globe by powerful winds, changing Earth's weather for several years. The volcano's explosion and collapse also generated deadly tsunami waves that destroyed the coastlines of Java and Sumatra and killed almost 36,000 Indonesians. As the waves spread outward from Indonesia, they destroyed the harbor in Perth, Australia; smashed riverboats in Calcutta, India; and even raised the tides in the English Channel more than halfway around the world.

The Great Chilean Earthquake of 1960 was the strongest quake ever recorded, with a magnitude of 9.5 on the Richter scale. Tsunami waves spread out from the earthquake's center and swept across the Pacific Ocean, pounding Hawaii with 35-foot waves about 15 hours later and continuing on to the shores of Japan. Estimates of the number of people killed by the quake and resulting tsunami vary from 490 to 2,290.

The Indian Ocean earthquake in 2004 had a magnitude of 9.15 on the Richter scale and unleashed a series of massive tsunamis that killed an estimated 230,000 people, making it the deadliest tsunami disaster in history. People died in areas ranging from near the quake in Indonesia, Thailand, and Malaysia to thousands of miles away on the shores of eastern Africa.

Dense fog can be a death trap for aircraft pilots, ship captains, and motorists. Many plane accidents in particular result from flying into heavy fog. To help pilots fly and land in dense fog, it's critical that airports have the most effective signaling lights possible. In this challenge, finalists confronted a chamber filled with dense fog to simulate a fogged-in airport.

As they peered into the gloom, the judges gave them their assignment: You are challenged to determine which color and frequency of light can best shine through dense fog. Using the signaling lights provided, test the lights with color filters that change the frequency of the light waves. As a control, first test the color filters in normal light. Then test them again in heavy fog conditions. To measure your results, you will use a light meter sensitive to tiny variations of light intensity.

Blind Spot

Team Blue got off to a strong start, with Neela Thangada leading the way. As the team brainstormed their approach, Neela suggested how best to proceed. They would first test the color filters in normal light, with each team member doing an assigned task.

As the team members picked their tasks, they suddenly ran into a blind spot—literally. Teammate Aaron Rozon was color-blind! If he couldn't see which color any of the filters were, how could he take part? Luckily, he found that he could read the gray and black light meter just fine. So, Aaron became the man on the meter, and Team Blue was back into action.

They all look the same to me.

Fogbound

Meanwhile, Team Purple was having a rough time. Deep into the challenge, the teammates were still debating different colors. Host J. D. Roth listened in.

"I think yellow and green are the best colors, because they look the brightest," said one teammate.

"No, yellow is much more visible than the green," said another.

"We should try the red filter again," said a third.

"Can you come up with an equation for these ideas, or are they trial and error?" asked J. D. "What's your method?"

"We're using some intuition and a little bit of trial and error," they said. As the minutes ticked away, Team Purple was still groping for answers.

Lighting the Way

Team Blue used the methodical approach of testing each color one by one. When the teammates weren't sure of the results, they retested to confirm the meter readings.

"Let's run yellow and orange again because their results are close," said Neela. "We want to be sure of our measurements."

Light Readings

As soon as all the readings were complete, Team Blue gathered around to analyze the data.

"Look at that," said Aaron. "Yellow doesn't change at all in the fog. It measured 9.5 in daylight, and it also measures 9.5 in the fog. And 9.5 is the highest fog rating!"

The team members all agreed: Yellow is the best color for signaling through fog.

David Caruso, one of the judges, was pleased with Team Blue. "You did careful work and reached the right conclusion," he said.

All Clear

Team Blue's strong communication skills, teamwork, and ability to solve problems earned them top marks in the Fog challenge. Team Gray came in a close second, with Team Yellow in third place. In the overall competition, Teams Blue and Gray were neck and neck for first.

Challenge 4

After a tsunami, tornado, or other natural disaster strikes, the people who survive the calamity face new dangers. Polluted water, spilled toxic waste, downed power lines, ruined homes, piles of rubble, and a lack of medical and food supplies confront survivors as they struggle to care for the wounded, bury the dead, and clean up the mess. Working in improvised clinics, the medics must safely encapsulate biohazards and other waste to prevent the spread of bacteria, viruses, and harmful chemicals.

In the Emergency challenge, finalists were confronted with a table covered with simulated medical waste, including bloody cotton pads, amputated body parts, and other gooey, stinky waste. Even though the mess was all fake, it looked and smelled disgusting.

As the teams stared at the waste, science host Dottie Klugel told them their assignment: You are challenged to act as medical technicians, devising tools and techniques for the safe encapsulation of infectious medical waste. You are restricted to the use of materials from the disaster site. You will be judged on how safely you encapsulate one cubic foot of solid and liquid medical waste.

Waste Not

One of the toughest parts of this challenge was figuring out how to clean up the contaminated waste using the few items the teams had to work with: oil drums, trash bags and food containers, household items (hammers, pliers, clothes hangers, string, boards), hazardous materials (haz-mat) suits and sterile gear for protection, empty biohazard boxes and warning stickers.

The teams had to not only clean up all the waste, but also get rid of any tools that got contaminated. While they worked, they had to keep themselves as clean as possible. And the clock was ticking, with only 90 minutes to get the job done.

 Oops!

Sticking Point

Team Red got off to the fastest start, pulling on protective gear and whirling into action. With Taylor Jones leading the way, the team started scraping up the mess, using hangers and one of the long sticks as scraping tools. The long stick worked well—until they tried to put it into their containment box and discovered it was much too long to fit inside!

Contaminated!

Meanwhile, Team Gold looked over their materials. "Let's not use the big sticks, because they'll stick out of the box," said Melanie Kabinoff. "If we use the hangers as tools, they'll fit inside." Her teammates agreed, and they scraped up goo and gauze pads, pushed an "amputated foot" into an empty food bag, and packed everything into their biohazard box. When they were finished, Dottie switched on the UV light to reveal the fluorescent powder that stood in for germs.

"Ick, the stuff is everywhere," said Joanna Guy.

"How do you think you did?" asked Dottie.

"There's a lot of contamination," said Nilesh Tripuraneni.

Yuck!

Cleaning Up Their Act

Team Gold was determined to make a clean sweep on their second try. As they worked, they kept track of what was clean and what wasn't. "Don't put that down over there," said Nilesh. "That surface has been wiped clean already."

After the team filled and sealed their box the second time, Dottie turned on the UV light again. This time, Team Gold saw much less contamination. "Very nice job," said Dottie, smiling.

Box Score

When the results were in, Team Gold had come in first. Team Gray was a close second, and third place went to Team Red. In a big upset, Team Blue came in fourth, hurting its chances for the overall team prize.

Science Skills Challenges

After the Forces of Nature theme challenges, the teams competed in two more events. These additional challenges tested lab skills in a series of timed activities.

Chemistry Classic

Extreme chemistry—that's what this challenge was about. The finalists were challenged not only to demonstrate the iodine clock reaction, a classic "surprise" experiment, by mixing two colorless chemical solutions, but also to do it in time to a piece of music. If the finalists did the experiment correctly, a surprising color change occurred in the liquid—and if they timed it well, the change would occur right at a dramatic point in the music.

Lab Tech Relay

This challenge tested basic lab skills and knowledge of chemistry, physics, biology, and geology. The finalists had to complete eight standard lab operations in a relay race, working with precision and accuracy. And, of course, they had only 90 minutes to complete the relay. The skills tested included using a balance to determine mass, classifying rocks and minerals, measuring liquids of varying densities, separating solids of different densities, assembling an electrical circuit, and using a microscope to identify slides.

The Winners

Now the judges faced their own challenge: selecting the winners from a terrific group of finalists. "The contestants for the Forces of Nature challenge have been outstanding," said Steven Jacobs, head judge. "It's exciting to judge such a talented group of young scientists."

First Prize
Neela Thangada
San Antonio, Texas

"And first place goes to . . . Neela Thangada!" When asked to comment on Neela's victory, the judges praised her team leadership, ability to solve science problems, and superb communication skills. Neela received a $20,000 scholarship and the title of America's Top Young Scientist of the Year.

For her science project, Neela studied plant cloning. She chose this topic because she wants to learn how to increase crop production in countries where there is not enough food. Plant cloning, she believes, could become an important food source in the future. (For more information on Neela's science project, see page 68.) In her free time, Neela enjoys playing sports and reading. Her career goal is to become a professor of medicine. "Both teaching and medicine help people, and that is my dream," she said.

Second Prize
Nilesh Tripuraneni
Fresno, California

Nilesh won second place and a $10,000 scholarship for his excellent science project and his fine performance during the team competition. His project, Solar Production of Hydrogen from Seawater via Electrolysis, featured an environmentally friendly approach to producing hydrogen by using solar power. (To read more about Nilesh's project, see page 73.)

Nilesh likes to play the guitar, make pottery, and compete on his school's math team. He hopes to become a geochemist because "the sheer power and complexity of the Earth captivates me."

Third Prize
Mary Lou Hedberg
North Attleboro, Massachusetts

As third prize winner, Mary Lou Hedberg took home a $5,000 scholarship. She earned high scores both for her science project and her leadership during the team competition. Mary Lou's science project was titled Paddle Perfection and featured a new, more efficient paddle for kayaks that she designed and tested. (For more information on Mary Lou's project, see page 75.) Her new design is so innovative that Mary Lou has filed a patent application for it. For her future career, Mary Lou hopes to become an engineer.

Team Award

When the judges announced the team scores, Team Gray came out on top. For their victory they received the National Park Service Explorer Award. The teammates—left to right: Alexander Uribe, Colleen Ryan, Anudeep Gosal, Elijah Mena, and Iftin Abshir—would travel to Mesa Verde National Park and work with scientists and national park researchers to study 3-D archaeological imaging. The judges praised the group for shared initiative, cooperation, and collaboration.

2 It's All About PHYSICS

Put together 40 whiz kids, four exciting challenges, and the groundbreaking theories of one 20th-century science genius. What do you have? It's All About Physics—a tribute to some of the most original theories of renowned physicist Albert Einstein and the theme for the 2004 *Discovery Channel Young Scientist Challenge.*

Albert Einstein

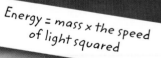

$$E = mc^2$$

Energy = mass x the speed of light squared

A galaxy's gravitational field warps distant starlight

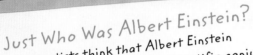

Just Who Was Albert Einstein?

Many scientists think that Albert Einstein (1879–1955) was the greatest scientific genius of the 20th century. In the space of one short year—1905—Einstein published a number of important scientific papers, some of which would forever change our thinking about how the world works.

Ideas Developed by Einstein in 1905:

- THE SPECIAL THEORY OF RELATIVITY

- AN EXPLANATION OF THE PHOTOELECTRIC EFFECT—THE START OF QUANTUM PHYSICS, OR THE PHYSICS OF THE ATOM

- THE NOTION THAT THE SPEED OF LIGHT IS ABSOLUTE, BUT THAT SPACE AND TIME ARE NOT

- $E=MC^2$, OR THE STATEMENT THAT ENERGY AND MASS ARE EQUIVALENT

- PROOF THAT MOLECULES ARE REAL

After presenting their science projects, the finalists were divided into eight teams and were joined on the scene by Jamie Hyneman and Adam Savage, hosts of the popular *MythBusters* TV series on Discovery Channel. What followed was an exhibition of classic scientific theories—gone extreme!

*I*magine you're standing on a platform watching two trains pass by in opposite directions. Both trains are traveling at 30 miles per hour. Now imagine that you're the engineer in one of the trains. Are the trains still approaching one another at the same speed?

Does the speed of a moving object change depending on where the observer is located? In other words, is speed, or motion, relative? That's what Albert Einstein was thinking about when he developed his special theory of relativity. According to his theory, a moving vehicle clocked at one speed when observed by someone standing still (the absolute speed) would be clocked at a totally different speed when observed by someone or something in motion (the relative speed). In the Radar Gun Luge challenge, the Young Scientist teams would put Einstein's theory to the test.

Gearing Up

For this challenge, the teams would send small carts hurtling down 300-foot parallel tracks in opposite directions. First, the teams would measure each cart's absolute speed as it whizzed by a team member holding a radar gun. Based on the absolute speed of each cart, the teams had to predict the relative speed of the two carts as they sped past each other in opposite directions. Then, with one cart carrying a radar gun, the teams would measure the carts' relative speed.

Quick Draw—Not!

The radar guns, it turned out, were not that easy to use. Sometimes team members held the guns at the wrong angle, making it difficult to register the correct speed consistently. Sometimes the radar guns didn't register the speed at all. And sometimes the problem was simpler—the radar gun hadn't been turned on!

I'll never make a traffic cop!

Think About It

A thought experiment is an attempt to solve a practical problem by using an analogy, or by comparing it with a hypothetical situation. Albert Einstein used a thought experiment about two trains passing in opposite directions when he developed the special theory of relativity. However, Galileo is the first scientist known to have used thought experiments to prove his theories. One of Galileo's thought experiments led him to state that Earth revolved on its axis and orbited the Sun.

Yes, I'm gonna be a star!

Speed 101

Jon Reasoner of Team Yellow not only found a college textbook on physics to help understand the challenge but also got the right angle on it—literally! He discovered that only by facing a moving cart head-on could he get accurate (and repeatedly reliable) measurements of its absolute speed. It didn't work to aim the radar gun at the side of the cart as it whizzed by. Team Yellow measured each cart's absolute speed at just over 30 miles per hour.

We've Got It!

After some discussion and experiment with the radar guns, Team Yellow predicted that the relative speed of the carts would equal the absolute speed of each cart added together. Now all they had to do was prove it!

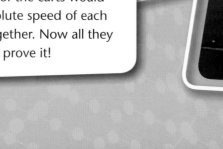

Gotcha!

Let 'er rip!

Relative Success

With the working radar gun in place on one cart, the teammates sent the carts racing down the tracks—and learned that the carts' relative speed was a whopping 63 miles per hour! Team Yellow had proved their hypothesis that the relative speed of the carts would be their combined absolute speeds.

Falling into Place

A combination of teamwork, excellent communication skills, and the leadership of math whiz David Westrich landed Team Gray in first place. Team Green took second, while despite their good work, Team Yellow came in third.

Good Thinking

In 1905, Albert Einstein published his paper about the special theory of relativity, which included his thoughts on motion. It took him five weeks to develop these ideas. However, the paper only dealt with the motion of objects at a steady speed along a straight line—thus, the word "special" in the title. It took Einstein four years to develop his general theory of relativity, which would include all motion.

Even though skateboarding and stunt bike–riding weren't around when Einstein was a child, he would have been fascinated by the sports. After all, Einstein's work on gravity and acceleration was an important piece of his general theory of relativity. It's what enabled him to take his theory about uniform motion and expand it to cover all kinds of motion.

The Skateboard Physics challenge was all about gravity. It challenged finalists to ask: Where does a skateboarder or a biker feel the most gravity? The least gravity? Team members would watch some very cool tricks on a half-pipe ramp performed by expert skateboarders and BMX bikers. Then they'd get to use a roller coaster model to help them figure out how to predict where the athletes would feel the most gravity (maximum g's) or the least gravity (zero g's). Once the team members made their predictions, they'd use high-tech gadgets like accelerometers, motion sensors, and digital video cameras to verify their ideas.

Expert Advisors

Team Green's first order of business was to build a successful model to plot out the athletes' path. The model roller coaster would help. The curved track could represent the half pipe, and the marble, the skateboarder or biker. But where to start with their predictions? After Team Green's Shannon McClintock asked the athletes about the forces they felt at the apex of their turn and along the straight stretch of the half pipe, the teammates had a better idea where to begin.

What's up with that?

On a Roll

Meanwhile, Team gray was having trouble understanding exactly what gravity was all about. Then MythBusters' Jamie weighed in with these questions: "What do you think is really happening here? Is this more about gravity, or is it more about a change in direction?"

What's Up with Gravity?

Gravity is the force that made an apple fall from a tree and bonk Isaac Newton on the head. Actually, it's doubtful that the apple really hit Newton, but the fall of an apple did get him thinking. He realized something special about the force that pulls an apple to the ground when it falls. It's really the force of attraction between two objects—in this case, the apple and the ground. From there, he was able to figure out that this same attraction is what keeps the Earth in orbit around the sun.

Is That the Question?

That was the question that seemed to turn things around for all the teams. They suddenly realized that the split second when the athlete was airborne and had gotten as high as he could before he started to fall back was the key. Team Gray's David Westrich quickly zeroed in on the issue when he asked the athletes whether they felt weightless just before or just after the turn. The athletes' answer: It happened at the same time.

Totally over the top!

Swinging It Around

Team Green got creative by taking one of the motion sensors and swinging it on its cord like a pendulum. Shannon McClintock gave Kyle Yawn credit for perfecting the idea, saying it "really helped in simulating what was happening in the half pipe." The teammates hooked the swinging sensor up to the computer, which allowed them to predict the zero g and maximum g points with certainty before putting their ideas to the test with the actual athletes.

The Real Test

Once the motion sensor was hooked up to an athlete, Team Green was ready to film the skater and test the data. It worked! The computer model generated by their pendulum matched up with the data from the athletes perfectly: The maximum g's occurred just after the skater's moment of apparent weightlessness at the apex of his run.

You got it!

Skating to Victory

In this challenge, Team Green put their communication skills to work and took first place, while Team Gray came in second, followed by Team Yellow. Everyone was impressed with the finalists—especially the athletes. One skateboarder said, "Maybe if we knew about this years ago, we'd be skating better!"

Did You Know?

In physics, acceleration refers to the change in how fast something is moving, regardless of whether it's speeding up or slowing down.

Einstein and Gravity

In his special theory of relativity, Albert Einstein dealt only with uniform motion. For example, imagine you're on an airplane flying at a steady 500 miles per hour. If the shades are pulled down over all the windows, how can you tell that you're moving? The answer is you can't. You pour yourself a glass of water, walk down the aisle, or wash your hands exactly the same way you can when you're in your own home. However, if the plane is taking off, flying through turbulent air, or slowing down for a landing, the plane has moved from uniform motion to accelerated motion—and you'd feel the movement even if all the window shades were down. Einstein wanted to extend his theory to cover accelerated motion.

Here's another thought experiment. Imagine you're inside a rocket ship. You're so far out in space that you no longer feel the effects of Earth's gravitation, and you seem weightless as you float around the ship. Now the captain ignites the engines, which are at the bottom, and the rocket ship starts to move. As the acceleration increases, the floor above the engines pushes up against you. If the acceleration of the rocket ship peaked at one g and you didn't know you were out in space, you'd feel the same way you would if you were on Earth. Only this time, you're not experiencing gravity, you're feeling the effects of acceleration. Einstein's realization that gravity and the effects of acceleration are equivalent led to the formulation of his general theory of relativity.

Challenge 3

During Albert Einstein's milestone year of 1905, the paper for which he won the Nobel Prize was the one that explained the photoelectric effect—the science behind photocells that convert sunlight into electricity. His ideas on the subject became the basis for quantum physics, or the physics of the atom. They also laid the groundwork for the development of the laser many years later.

This inspired the creation of the Laser Obstacle Course challenge. The teams were asked to use a number of mirrors angled just so to bounce a laser beam under a limbo bar, through a small hole in the center of a target, through a long pipe, and off a ceiling-mounted mirror to hit a final target with absolute precision. They could use a low-power beam to help them map out their course. Then they'd turn on the high-power beam for the final run. If their practice run wasn't precise, the high-power beam would burn the obstacles and points would be deducted from their scores.

The Path of Light

It was a race against time to blaze a path of light around the obstacle course. All the teams were in a hurry to get moving. They were full of ideas. Too full of ideas, actually. Team Yellow struggled with their strategy. They couldn't quite figure out how best to position the mirrors to hit all their targets.

Light in Time

Team Green had a really cool idea, but leader Shannon McClintock said that when they sketched it out, "We found out that we actually didn't have enough mirrors for that. We might have wasted half of our challenge time going through with that, only to find out we had to start over."

Getting the Light Angle

Luckily, Jamie Hyneman and Adam Savage were on hand. Jamie's advice to Team Red: "Try and organize this into something that's systematic. Think of it in terms of right, left, up, and down." The idea of doing the most with the fewest angles began to sink in.

Green's Secret Weapon

By then, Team Green was already on the right track. "Before we ever do a challenge, we sit down and we plan," said Blake Thompson, who earned the title of Team Green's secret weapon.

Shannon said, "Blake is definitely a good listener. He always waits until everyone else has got their ideas on the table, and then he'll think about everything that's been brought out and he'll give his idea."

Finding the Way

With Blake's help, Team Green quickly established that the simplest route around the course was a large, rectangular shape. And when they had trouble with the final obstacle, it was Blake who took charge. He realized that the pipe was too big to move easily, so he suggested adjusting the mirror instead.

On the Beam

Team Green was finally ready for the test. Everything was lined up. Now it was time to stand back, kick on the big laser, and . . . bull's-eye! The teammates were right on target—and in only half the allotted time! Team Green shot into first place on the Laser challenge, while second place went to Team Orange and third place to Team Red.

One of Einstein's famous papers dealt with the motion of molecules. In the Teeth on Edge: A Real Screech challenge, the finalists were given a chance to honor this work by exploring vibrations—the molecular motion of sound itself.

The teams were shown a variety of very unusual instruments—including an armonica (above), which is a collection of glass bowls that rotate on a spindle, and an LSI (that's long-stringed instrument to you and me). The judges told the teams: Start with the theme of Beethoven's Fifth Symphony and apply your own experiences and personalities to create something that is uniquely your own, perform the piece, and record your performance.

Making Music

The members of Team Yellow had all taken music lessons before, and they went for a classical approach. "We started with the instruments that made the best melody," said Christine Johns, "and we just kept rolling them on top of each other until it sounded really great."

"We tried to put in a little of our own flair and tried to show our individuality," added Blake Zwerling.

Practice makes perfect!

Did You Know?

The armonica was invented by Benjamin Franklin in 1761. He mounted 37 glass bowls in graduated sizes on an iron spindle. To play it, he wet the bowls, pressed his fingers against the rims, and rotated the spindle with a foot treadle to produce a melody.

Beethoven's rolling in his grave!

Roll Over, Beethoven!

Team Gray chose unusual sounds to build an interpretation of the music that was truly expressive of themselves, making some interesting (if not beautiful) music together. For the finishing touch on their masterpiece, they chose a classic wind instrument: a whoopee cushion!

The High Notes

As the curtain came down on Team Gray's final performance, the scores came in. Team Gray had hit all the right notes and finished at the top of the scale. Team Orange captured second place, and Team Black finished third.

Science Skills Challenges

Two additional challenges—*Skulls Unlimited* and *Paramecium Rodeo*—were set before the finalists to evaluate their science process skills.

Skulls Unlimited

In this challenge, teams were shown a collection of bones (including complete skeletons) and asked to identify 40 of them within a certain time limit. The finalists were given clues and reference materials to help them with the identification process. Teams were then judged on how they worked together to get all the tasks done, how well they used the reference materials, and how they evaluated the clues.

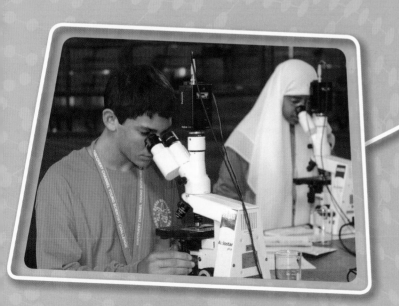

Paramecium Rodeo

This challenge got the finalists thinking about living specimens as opposed to skeletal remains. Teams were given the chance to use powerful technology to examine, identify, and then photograph a bevy of microscopic beasties. Judges looked at the clarity of the photographs the finalists took. They also looked at the methods each team used to round up and recognize microorganisms such as paramecia, daphnia, hydra, and more. Yee-haw! Git along, very little dogie!

The Winners

At last the big moment had arrived. "Every one of you could have won this thing. Every single one of you. It was that close," said head judge Steven Jacobs before announcing the individual winners and team award.

First Prize
Shannon McClintock
San Diego, California

In 2004, Shannon was named America's Top Young Scientist of the Year and received a $15,000 scholarship for her leadership, teamwork, and her presentation of her science project in which she showed that garnet grit helps trains get better traction than the more commonly used silica sand. (For more information on Shannon's project, see page 80.)

Shannon loves to read and write creatively. Her favorite hobbies include playing with her dog and playing on a field hockey team. A leader in both sports (she's captain of her team) and science, Shannon says that a relative who works for the Jet Propulsion Laboratory got her excited about science.

Second Prize
Blake Thompson
Gainesville, Florida

Planner, thinker, and bug guy. That's Blake Thompson, 2004's second place winner and $7,500 scholarship recipient. Blake is interested in everything around him—which is how he got interested in learning more about the fire ants that plague so many people in his hometown. (For more information on Blake's project, see page 72.)

Blake's ambition is to become an eco-friendly architect. He says, "This would allow me to use both my artistic skills and scientific knowledge."

Third Prize
David Westrich
Cape Girardeau, Missouri

David Westrich took third place, winning a $5,000 scholarship. For his science project, David investigated the effect of lead pollution on invertebrates living in the ground near a local smelter. (For more information on David's project, see page 78.)

David is your basic all-around teen. He enjoys reading and playing on the computer, he likes sports such as basketball and baseball, and he is a member of the school band. David says he would like to go into medicine "so that I can help find cures for disease." He considers his father, who has encouraged his interest in science, to be his mentor.

Team Award

When the judges announced the overall team scores, the winner was Team Gray, whose members were lauded for their science skills, teamwork, and communication skills. They won The National Park Service Team Award. The team—left to right: David Marash-Whitman, Celine Saucier, David Westrich, Sravya Keremane, and Julia Fanning—would travel to Grand Teton and Yellowstone National Parks to study wolves in the wild.

47

All About AVIATION

When the 40 finalists in the *Discovery Channel Young Scientist Challenge* met at Reagan National Airport in Washington, D.C., they were flying high. The year was 2003—100 years since Wilbur and Orville Wright made their historic launch of the first successful powered airplane flight at the dunes near Kitty Hawk, North Carolina.

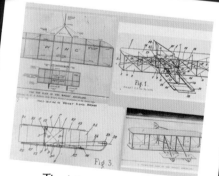

The first powered flight

The Wright brothers' patent plan sketches

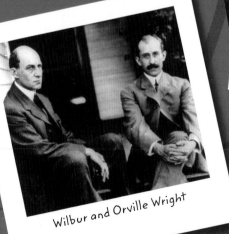

Wilbur and Orville Wright

The Wright Men for the Job

Wilbur and Orville Wright were the two youngest sons of Milton and Susan Wright. It was Susan who fostered a love of building and mechanics within the family. She'd been a top math student in college and, as a child, had liked helping her father in his workshop.

As a result, the Wright children were always taking things apart and putting them back together to see how they worked. When the boys were young, their father brought home a rubber band–powered toy that could lift itself into the air. That got them thinking about the mechanics of flight. So, years later when their thriving bicycle business gave them enough money to live comfortably, the brothers turned their thoughts back to flying. The brothers were already well known for building the best bikes around. Why shouldn't they have similar success with a flying machine?

On the morning of the first day, 40 of America's most promising middle grade scientists donned their flight suits and entered the giant doors of a hangar at the airport. After meeting with the judges, they divided into eight teams and prepared to tackle the challenges that would take them from the birth of aviation to the space age—in just 48 hours!

The Wright Stuff

Challenge 1

*T*he Wright brothers experimented with many wing designs before they launched their first flight. They also tested their designs in a wind tunnel. Could modern-day kids make workable wings of their own using tools from the turn of the 20th century? No computers were allowed—not even a ballpoint pen! The goal of each team was to design, build, and test as many wings as possible. Points were awarded only for wings that worked.

The fact that none of the students had any high school physics was their biggest challenge. They'd have to go with their intuitive feel for the physics of flight—which was more or less the position the Wright brothers were in—plus a crash course in the concepts of drag and lift from their judges, who also acted as science coaches. Of course, Wilbur and Orville had several years to perfect and test their designs. These teams had only 90 minutes!

50

Now this is a real challenge!

Design a Wing

Everyone got to work drawing up wing designs. But Team Black quickly learned that early 20th-century technology had its limits. "We got to use basically quills," said Joseph Stunzi. "So, in drafting your wing, you had to constantly try and get this pen to work."

Once that little challenge was conquered, the teammates all took turns soldering and using a hammer and mini-anvil to pound sheets of pliable copper into the shape of their designs.

Putting It to the Test

Meanwhile, Team Red was testing its model wings in the wind tunnel, a miniature version of the one the Wright brothers had built in 1901. The big difference was that this wind tunnel would be kid-powered! A bicycle set up on a stationary platform operated a flywheel that would make the wind. Air in the wind tunnel would move across the wings. If the wing lifted, it would pull on the counterweights connected to it. The more the wing moved, the more lift and the better the wing.

Air Pressure and Lift

Put simply, air pressure is the force produced by the motion of the air molecules in our atmosphere. Remember: Air is a gas, so it is easily blown around by wind. That means that sometimes there are more air molecules over one area. When that happens, the pressure increases because there is greater force per unit area. When there are fewer molecules grouped together—due to winds or higher elevations—there is lower pressure.

When air rushes over an arched surface, it moves faster and farther than the air passing beneath the wing. Bernoulli's principle (see page 13) sets forth the idea that when a fluid (either liquid or gas) moves faster, it experiences a decrease in pressure. So the faster air rushing over the curved top of a wing results in lower air pressure above that wing. The higher air pressure under the wing pushes the wing up. *Voila!* We have lift!

Back to the Drawing Board

Conscious of the ticking clock, Team Black mounted their wing models in the wooden testing box, while Joseph Stunzi mounted the bike that would work the fan to make the wind. In order to maintain the necessary constant wind speed, he had to pedal consistently.

"The hardest part is when you're counting your pedals, you have to make sure it's constant," Joseph said, "and you have to breathe at the same time."

And after all that hard work, the model wings didn't move with lift from the wind. It was back to the drawing board for Team Black.

Don't forget to breathe!

Light at the End of the Wind Tunnel

After a quick huddle on redesign, Team Black finally saw some success—their new designs worked! Their score was lower than they'd hoped because they only made two working models. But their judge was impressed by their engineering skills. "You guys are some fantastic model builders," he said. Team Black had great designs, just not enough of them.

Wright On!

Unlike Team Black, Team Yellow succeeded in making enough working wing designs to land them in first place in the Wright Stuff challenge. Team Orange was close behind, with Team Blue in third place. Team Black tied for fifth.

Not far from the airport setting of the All About Aviation challenge is the spot from which Orville Wright embarked on another historic flight in 1908. Unlike their previous flights, this one was witnessed by hundreds of onlookers and was the first to include a passenger. During their early flights, the Wright Brothers were constantly making mechanical adjustments as they had more experience with wind and weather conditions.

This inspired the Earth, Wind, and Glider challenge, where the teams of finalists were asked to assemble, modify, and fly rubber-band propelled gliders—large planes that can glide in the air for some distance—with three-foot wingspans. The teams were given partly built model gliders to complete as they saw fit. Then they'd test the gliders. Each team would be awarded points for how far their gliders flew—but they would lose points for every foot the gliders went off course.

Thinking Outside the Box

Team Yellow didn't trust the gliders as they came out of the box, so the teammates immediately set to work modifying them. They were allowed to use lead foil, paper clips, tape, and cutters to make the desired changes. Would the modifications allow for both straight and distance flight? With luck, there would be time enough to test the modified gliders and make adjustments.

Where does this go?

Nothing's Easy

No sooner did Team Yellow finally get a glider airborne than they ran into more trouble. "I threw it toward the side of the field where there was one single tree and a whole bunch of empty space," said Tony Burnetti, "and it got stuck in the one tree." After that, they adopted a simple strategy: Fly short, fly straight—and the team members took turns racking up points.

Seeing Red

Team Red members nailed their glider modifications immediately—their gliders were flying straight and long. The team was flying high, but the pilots found that they had to battle shifting winds. Teammate Elizabeth Monier had the answer. She suggested that they weight one model in front and the other in back. One model would be for throwing against the wind at a downward angle, which would allow the glider to slice through the wind instead of fighting against it. The other model was for throwing downwind at an upward angle in order to let the wind carry the glider as far as possible.

Gliding to the Finish

Team Red's two-plane strategy, teamwork, and communication skills paid off. They tied with Teams Blue, Green, and Black for first in the challenge and made the longest single flight of the day—167 feet!

Wilbur Wright

Getting It Wright

One reason the Wright brothers succeeded at inventing a flying machine was their scientific approach to the task. They systematically identified all the problems they needed to solve, and then discussed every possible solution they could think of. Eventually, they worked out three main issues. They had to 1) find a way to control the machine in flight; 2) design wings that would provide enough lift to carry the combined weight of the flyer, the engine, and a person; and 3) build a light engine with enough power to give thrust, or forward push, and carry the flyer along.

Wilbur hit upon the notion that they needed to raise and lower the wing tips—rather than the entire wing—to control the flight. The brothers worked out how to use wires to move the wing tips up and down. Wilbur called this innovation wing warping. To this day, many scientists consider the invention of wing warping to be the single most important contribution the Wright Brothers made to flight mechanics.

Fast-forward about 50 years to the beginning of the next major challenge in flight technology: manned flight in space. In the late 1950s, scientists in both the United States and Soviet Russia were racing to take German rocket technology to the next level. The rockets that the Nazis used to such great effect against the British during World War II (1939–1945) were the very same rockets used to jumpstart America's first space program. Suddenly, what had been a devastating development in long-range weaponry was transformed into the cornerstone of man's first attempt to enter space, the final frontier.

The Rocket Cars challenge took its inspiration from the space race. In this challenge, students were asked to safely engineer their own rocket car launch. They had to modify a go-cart powered by a supersized fire extinguisher holding less than 30 seconds of carbon dioxide (CO_2) fuel. The goal was to get as far as they could down and back a 600-foot test track.

Rocket Power

Each team was provided with just enough fuel for two runs, one test and one final. It was the teammates' job to figure out how much air to put in the tires, how to ration their fuel, and how to pick the right nozzle—too small and they wouldn't go fast enough; too large and they might waste fuel. They had to balance the need for speed plus momentum (the force of forward motion) with the need for enough fuel to go the distance.

Know Your Nozzle

In their haste to hit the track, Team Red rushed through the planning stage, deciding it would be best to conserve as much fuel as possible. Choosing the smallest nozzle for their test, they went nowhere—slowly! "It may be because of the nozzle we used," said Elizabeth Monier. So they moved on to the midsize nozzle, with similar results. And this time, they'd exhausted their fuel supply.

Bummer!

How Rockets Work

Rocket science is quite different from the science behind airplane flight. Rocketry has other challenges to meet, such as how to break free of the enormous pull of Earth's gravity. To solve that problem, scientists looked back at Newton's third law of motion. In that law, Newton stated that for every action, there is an equal and opposite reaction. The trick was to find a force so powerful that its opposite reaction could blast a rocket from Earth's surface right out of the atmosphere. The solution scientists came up with was to use the tremendous force produced by exhaust gases from burning propellant, or fuel, ejected from the tail end of a rocket.

Go, Green!

Team Green was luckier. They spent more time at the drawing board, and they were certain that they'd worked out most of the kinks. Their plan engineered for power: They'd use the biggest nozzle for maximum thrust and ration their fuel by starting off with a full-throttle, seven-second burst to see how far it would take them. But the plan also required perfect timing on the part of the pilot.

"I'm really nervous," said David Edwards. "If I mess up, the whole team goes down." The burst worked to get David moving quickly, but he had to keep using fuel to reach the end. Would he have enough fuel to get back? Finally, the team decided to throw caution to the wind and told David to use it all. It worked! He made it back, with fuel to spare!

The Finish Line

Team Green did a good job in the Rocket Cars challenge but only tied for fourth place. Team Blue, however, put their heads together and came up with the perfect formula to finish first. Following close behind were Team Orange in second and Team Gray in third.

Super Sonic Tonic
Challenge 4

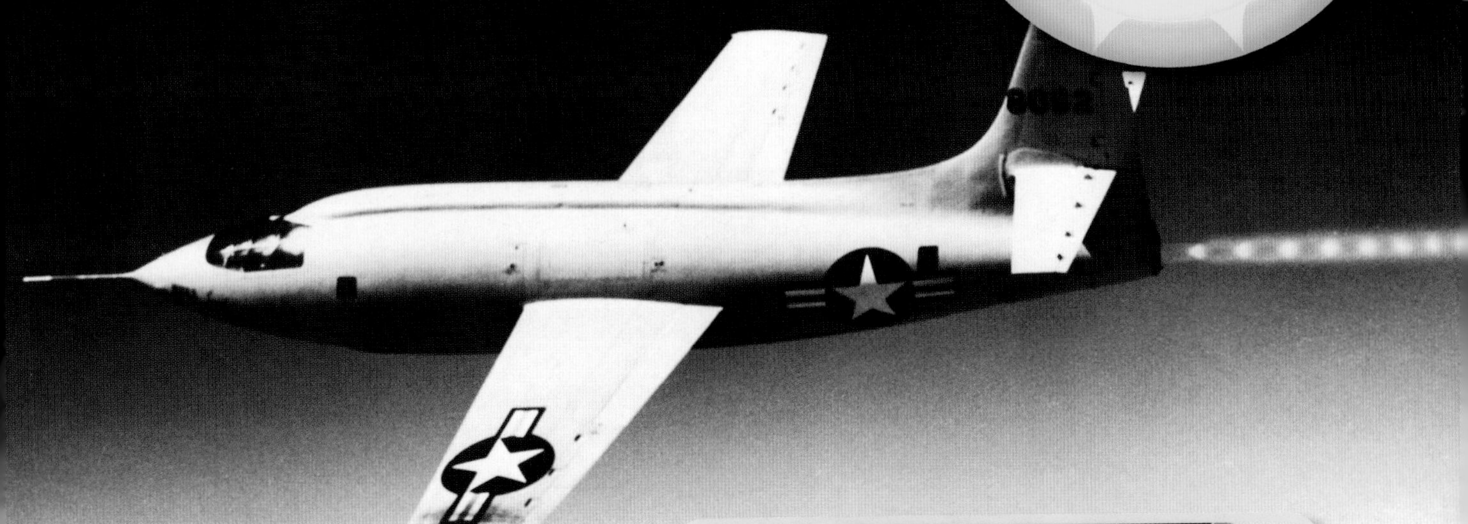

WARNING:
DO NOT TRY THIS AT HOME

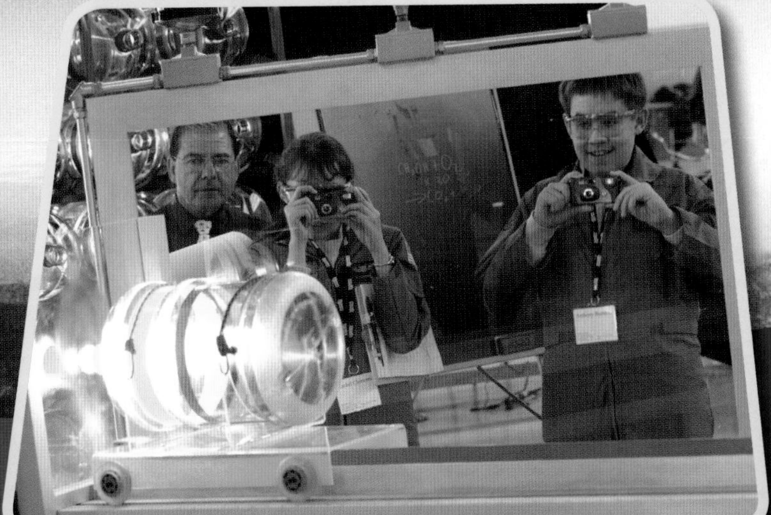

Day two began with a bang. In Super Sonic Tonic, a salute to the challenges faced by test pilot Chuck Yeager, finalists were asked to try a bit of fuel mixology. Yeager flew alcohol-and-air-fueled rocket planes, precursors to the rockets that would eventually take us into space.

The students were provided with five types of alcohol. They'd have to test each type to decide which would work best to shoot 5-gallon water drums down a 60-foot track. The catch: They could use only two spoonfuls to do it.

Note: This type of experiment should only be done in a closed lab under adult supervision!

Testing, Testing . . .

First came the testing phase. The teammates lit each fuel and made their observations. Some alcohols burned faster than others. Some burned more completely. Some burned hotter, as evident from the blue flame. Once the students settled on their fuel of choice, it was time to test it in action. That meant figuring out how to vaporize the liquid so it could ignite properly and send the water drum flying. But how? Shaking the liquid around and letting it evaporate on its own simply took too long.

Eureka!

For Team Yellow, Jeff Luttrell came to the rescue! Using a hair dryer, he heated the alcohol quickly and vaporized it. All that was left to do was ignite it and see what happened. With a flip of a switch, an electric igniter lit the gas and—BANG! The water jug shot down the track.

Said Jeff afterward, "Science is just trying things. You never know when something's going to be a discovery or a total failure."

Touchdown

With the right mix of teamwork, science skills—and fuel—Team Yellow shot into first place in the Super Sonic Tonic challenge. Team Green came in a close second, followed by Team Red in third place.

We've come a long way since the early days of flight. The latest developments in aviation technology can transform our lives. For instance, tiny remote-controlled micro aerial vehicles (MAV) are being developed that can help locate trapped victims in collapsed buildings. It takes special skills to fly these vehicles, which operate according to different laws of physics due to their small size and weight.

The finalists were given a kit for a remote-controlled spy-copter called the Draganflyer IV. Their assignment: Build the helicopter then master the principles of small-scale vehicle flight, piloting the craft accurately and landing it on a series of targets—all without an instruction manual. The team that made the most successful landings within the time limit would get the most points.

Preparing the copter for flight was a real challenge! How should they assemble the rotors? Which edge was the front? Which was the back? All the teams struggled with the assembly. The time was flying by, but not the copter. When the vehicle got launched at last, the teams' problems were only half over. They still had to learn how to land the copter so that it balanced properly and touched down flat. In the end, Team Black landed in first, Team Yellow touched down in second, and Teams Blue and Green tied for third.

The Winners

"It's such a delight to see that spark when it fires in the eyes of our finalists," said head judge Steven Jacobs. "It's what all science educators dream of seeing." The time had come to announce the individual winners and the team prize.

First Prize
Joseph Stunzi
Watkinsville, Georgia

Meet Joseph Stunzi, 2003's Top Young Scientist of the Year, comedian, and . . . mummy's boy? This amateur Egyptologist works hard and is good at nearly everything he tries, from playing the piano to finding the fun in everyday situations. But it was his real mother (not his mummy) who helped him to focus on his award-winning science project.

   Joseph's mother has arrhythmia and wears a pacemaker to help her heart beat normally. When Joseph's dad used to bring home his work—new cell phone technology—she complained about it giving her weird sensations. Joseph decided to learn more about how electronic emissions affect heart patients like his mother. (For more information on Joseph's project, see page 79.) His ambition is to become an electrophysiologist "because they implant pacemakers, help in fixing electrical problems in the heart, and meet new people every day."

Second Prize
Elizabeth Monier
Boerne, Texas

A can-do attitude and a keen, questioning mind are what distinguished Elizabeth Monier during the 2003 Challenge. It's also what distinguished her science project, which investigated the antimicrobial properties of untreated honey versus treated honey. (For more information on Elizabeth's project, see page 67.)

   Elizabeth enjoys playing sports like volleyball and softball, playing the piano, and doing volunteer work. She also helps out on her school's literary magazine, and she likes to read and hike. She hopes one day to pursue a career in the field of genetics, because she believes "it is essential to the development of human health standards."

Third Prize
Elena Ovaitt
Weston, Missouri

Elena Ovaitt is your regular small-town girl. She loves everything about her hometown, including the locally made drink, apple cider. What makes cider different from apple juice is that cider is not heated, so it can't be pasteurized for purity. Elena had read about purification of food using ozone (a process called ozonation), and she thought that it might kill off unwanted bacteria without turning the cider into juice. (For more information on Elena's project, see page 67.)

She has a keen eye for the practical uses of science and technology and wants to be a medical research scientist. "I find it exciting to discover new things," Elena says, "and I would like those scientific discoveries to benefit others."

Team Award
Teamwork, excellent communication skills, and strong science skills made Team Green—left to right: Jacob Rucker, Sarah Gerin, Spencer Larson, Luis Lafer-Sousa, and David Edwards—the highest scoring team of the 2003 Challenge.

In this chapter you'll find descriptions of the winning science projects of 40 Discovery Channel Young Scientist Challenge finalists.

Behavioral Science

Leading the Election:
Election Corruption Through Profiling
Dustin Shea and Jordan Pennell
Jacksonville, Illinois
Finalists, 2004

Background: Just how susceptible are people to subliminal advertising and marketing, which tries to influence people without their realizing it, even in making political decisions? That was the question two young political scientists posed with their mock election. Dustin and Jordan knew that information on personal likes and dislikes—profiling—is collected by marketers online. Can that information be used to influence our thinking on important matters like elections?

Methods and Results: Dustin and Jordan staged a mock election with two groups of students. The control group was asked to choose between two unknown candidates and was given plain white paper ballots. The profiled group was first tested for their favorite and least favorite colors. Then they were asked to vote for the same two unknown candidates. The difference was that each individual in the profiled group got special color ballots, according to their personal preferences. The candidate Dustin and Jordan were secretly supporting went on people's favorite colors; the other name went on their least favorite colors. The control group's vote was evenly split. But the profiled group went for Dustin and Jordan's candidate by a 25 percent margin!

You Are Getting Sleepy:
Sleep Habits in Children with ADHD
Mary Anne Messer
Hattiesburg, Mississippi
Finalist, 2004

Background: Mary Anne Messer noticed that her teenage brother's sleep habits changed as he got older. That got her thinking about children and sleep habits in general. To help her understand sleep better, she developed a survey, one that included a question to identify kids with Attention Deficit Hyperactivity Disorder (ADHD). It turns out that there were lots of them in the group of third and fourth graders she surveyed. Would the survey turn up differences in their sleep habits, known as "sleep hygiene"?

Methods and Results: Parents of 125 children responded to Mary Anne's survey. While most of the children had regular bedtimes and slept soundly through the night, the kids with ADHD—about 12 percent of the total—showed differences that were consistent throughout the group. On the whole, ADHD children were less likely to have a regular bedtime, fall asleep easily, or sleep soundly. That leaves Mary Anne with interesting questions: Do these children have different sleep habits because of their ADHD? Or is their ADHD more of a problem because of their sleep habits? She hopes, one day, to answer these questions.

Behavioral Science

Biochemistry

How Do You Like Your Eggs?
A Study of the Variation in Cholesterol Content of a Chicken's Egg Following Controlled Dietary Alterations
Heather Foster
Beverly Hills, Florida
Finalist, 2005

Background: Because of people's health concerns about high cholesterol, Heather decided to study cholesterol in eggs. She hypothesized that feeding chickens a raw vegetable diet would decrease the cholesterol content of their eggs.

Methods and Results: Heather chose a Rhode Island Red hen for her experiment. Over three weeks, she fed the hen four different diets: commercial feed, bananas with diced peels, soy meal, and raw vegetables. She kept the hen on each diet for five consecutive days. After five days, she took the last egg laid in that period and analyzed it, using a measurement instrument called a gas chromatograph. Heather found that the "soy egg"—the egg laid after the soy diet—had the least cholesterol: 31 percent less than a typical egg.

A Germicidal Light Zaps the Bugs That Bite
Taylor Jones
Maryville, Tennessee
Finalist, 2005

Background: When Taylor's grandmother became ill, her doctor said the cause may have been bacteria from soda cans purchased from a vending machine. Taylor decided to research the amount of bacteria found on soda cans. He formed the hypothesis that snacks and soda cans exposed to a germicidal light would have fewer bacteria on their surfaces than those taken straight from a vending machine and not exposed to a germicidal light.

Methods and Results: Taylor collected 13 snack packages and soda cans from vending machines. He took these samples to a university laboratory, swabbed each sample, and incubated the swabs. After incubation, he counted the number of bacterial colonies from each sample and did a test to identify the different types of bacteria (*E. coli* was one type he found). Next, he exposed the samples to germicidal light for different amounts of time, then reswabbed and incubated the new swabs. He found that 60 minutes of exposure to germicidal light killed 100 percent of the bacteria. After further research, he found that the exposure time needed to kill all the bacteria could be reduced by using a higher-wattage bulb.

Biochemistry

Biochemistry

Alternative Therapies for Advanced Stage Melanoma in Lumbricus terrestris

Melanie Kabinoff
Boynton Beach, Florida
Winner: Educator Award, 2005

Background: Melanie became interested in treatments for melanoma (skin cancer) when a former teacher developed the disease. She interviewed 40 melanoma patients and found that many of them had tried alternatives to the traditional treatments of radiation and chemotherapy. Melanie decided to research some of these alternative treatments.

Methods and Results: Melanie used a light chamber to expose yellow earthworms (*Lumbricus terrestris*) to the ultraviolet B (UV-B) radiation found in daylight, which causes melanoma. The worms exposed to the most radiation developed stage two and three melanoma cell growth. Melanie then immersed some of these worms in five liquids that have shown promise in reducing melanoma growth in humans: vitamin D, coffee, echinacea, tree oil, and soy milk. After 20 weeks of regular immersions, all the treated worms showed some decrease in melanoma cells. The worms treated with tree oil and echinacea showed the greatest decrease. In contrast, the untreated worms showed an increase in melanoma cells.

Garlic: It's Not Just for Vampires Anymore
The Effects of Processed Garlic on Antibiotic-Resistant Bacteria

Amanda Lu
Plano, Texas
Finalist, 2004

Biochemistry

Background: Amanda's mother is always telling her to eat more garlic. She says garlic is why Amanda's 80-something grandmother rarely gets sick. That got Amanda thinking: Is it really the garlic? And how effective is garlic in reducing bacteria, even after it's been cooked, digested, or both?

Methods and Results: Amanda decided to test garlic on different types of bacteria: nonresistant *E. coli*, ampicillin-resistant *E. coli*, and kanamycin-resistant *E. coli*. (Ampicillin and kanamycin are both antibiotics, medicines developed to kill bacteria. Some bacteria have become resistant to these antibiotics.) Amanda knew that allicin, the main antibacterial component in garlic, begins to degrade after cooking, so she was betting raw garlic would work better than cooked, and that nonresistant *E. coli* would have the fewest defenses against the herb. She placed raw and cooked garlic in separate containers with a mix of saliva, hydrochloric acid, pepsin, and sodium hydroxide—all of which are used in digestion. After filtering the pulp for unwanted bacteria, she placed samples on agar plates with the different bacteria strains and incubated them overnight. When the results were in, Amanda learned that, in this case, mother really does know best! The garlic was most effective on the nonresistant bacteria, but it also worked on the resistant strains. Raw garlic worked best, but even cooked garlic was effective.

Biochemistry

A Sticky Business
Antimicrobial Capabilities of Honey
Elizabeth Monier
Boerne, Texas
Winner: Second Place, 2003

Background: Elizabeth had read about using raw honey as an antibiotic. She was also aware of the recent increase in antibiotic-resistant bacteria. She wondered if honey would be a good natural alternative to drugs that were fast outliving their usefulness.

Methods and Results: Elizabeth tested her hypothesis in two phases. The first phase involved using dilutions of raw honey in varying strengths. She made four solutions of honey diluted with distilled water. Then, to kill off unwanted bacteria, she used heat, ultraviolet light, or ethanol (a type of alcohol) on three of the solutions. The fourth she left untreated. Next, Elizabeth combined the solutions with bits of chicken or beef and plated them with nutrient agar. The second phase involved testing undiluted raw honey under identical conditions. While lab conditions caused the results of her first phase to be inconclusive, the second phase went well. Elizabeth's conclusions: Undiluted raw honey is an effective antibiotic, but it loses its effectiveness with dilution or exposure to heat.

How Sweet It Is!
Purification by Ozonation
Elena Ovaitt
Weston, Missouri
Winner: Third Place, 2003

Background: Sure, pasteurization is a good thing, but is it always the right choice? Elena Ovaitt knew that when apple cider is pasteurized, the process causes the cider to lose a significant amount of vitamin C. What could be done to reduce bacteria colonies in cider yet preserve its vitamin content?

Methods and Results: Ozonation to the rescue! In Elena's town, ozonation—exposure to ozone (triatomic oxygen)—is used to purify water. Elena wondered if the process would work for cider. She applied four different amounts of ozone to cider and then measured the vitamin C and bacteria that remained. She found that the amounts of ozone she used did affect the bacteria. Next, she used mathematics to figure out the precise amount of ozone needed to remove all the bacteria. Elena's data also indicated that the ozonation process reduced the cider's vitamin C content by only 0.1 percent as compared to pasteurization's 33 to 50 percent reduction. How sweet success!

Biochemistry

The Proof Is in the Print:
An Analysis of Fingerprint Patterns Within Different Human Ethnicities
Iftin Abshir
Littleton, Colorado
Winner: Team Award, 2005

Background: Iftin became interested in fingerprints when she took a Junior Police Academy course. She decided to investigate if certain fingerprint patterns occur more often in some ethnic groups than in others. During her background research, she learned that the genes that determine fingerprint patterns and those that determine skin color are linked. Using that information, she developed her experiment.

Methods and Results: Iftin tested 40 people from five ethnicities: African, Asian, Caucasian, East Indian, and Latin American. She then classified each person's fingerprint by its main pattern: a whorl, a loop, or an arch. Her findings supported her hypothesis: The different ethnic groups showed clear differences in fingerprint patterns. For example, 67 percent of Latin American volunteers had loop patterns, compared with 50 percent of African volunteers. Similarly, 26 percent of African volunteers had arch patterns, whereas only 6 percent of East Indian volunteers had them.

Biochemistry

Botany

Effects of Various Nutrient Concentrations on the Cloning of the Eye of the *Solanum tuberosum* (potato) at Multiple Stages
Neela Thangada
San Antonio, Texas
Winner: First Place, 2005

Background: Neela's experiment was inspired by a biology textbook's description of potato cloning (in botany, reproduction by taking cuttings, which results in new plants that are genetically identical to the parent plant). From this source, she developed her own expanded cloning experiment, which was more complex in technique and scientific procedure. In her experiment, Neela wanted to find out how different concentrations of nutrients affect the stages of growth in a potato.

Methods and Results: First, Neela removed 60 shoot tips growing from potatoes. She then sterilized the tips and removed the bottom two segments, which are called the meristem and the primordial. Next, she placed the meristem, primordial, and remaining shoot tip segments into either a half-strength or full-strength nutrient medium. After several weeks, Neela found that the shoot tips in the full strength medium produced the most growth.

Will Silicon Help Plant Growth in South Florida Soils?

Kelsey Burnham
Okeechobee, Florida
Finalist, 2005

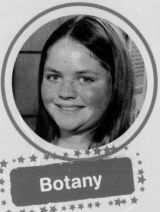

Botany

Background: Kelsey's father told her about a new silicon-based soil conditioner that he had learned about at an agricultural meeting. He said that studies had shown that this additive helps plants grow better and was interested in using it on their farms in southern Florida. (Silicon is a chemical element that makes up about 25 percent of the Earth's crust and is found in sand, quartz, and flint.) Kelsey devised an experiment to see if adding the silicon conditioner really would work. Her hypothesis was that plants given silicon and fertilizer would grow better than plants grown in plain soil or with fertilizer only.

Methods and Results: Kelsey planted oats in five testing groups, each consisting of three two-gallon pots. The pots in Group 1 had no additives at all. Those in Group 2 had a half-cup of silicon per gallon. Group 3 got no silicon but would have fertilizer added later. Group 4 had the same amount of silicon added as Group 2 but would also get fertilizer later. Group 5 had one cup of silicon added per gallon and would also get fertilizer later. Kelsey gave each pot the same amount of water. After four weeks, she clipped, dried, and weighed the oat plants, then did the same at the six-week mark and again at the nine-week mark. When she added up the weights for each group, she found that Group 2 grew better than Group 1; Groups 3, 4, and 5 grew better than Group 2; and Group 5 showed the most growth, which supported Kelsey's hypothesis.

Super Stevia:
Propagating Stevia Through Tissue Culture

Shireen Dhir
Kathleen, Georgia
Finalist, 2004

Background: Shireen Dhir's grandmother suffered from diabetes, a disease that prevents people from digesting sugars properly. Most diabetes patients have to restrict their sugar and carbohydrate intake, so Shireen understands the importance of a sugar substitute. Stevia, a shrub local to Paraguay, contains a natural sweetener that is safe for diabetics. The problem is that it reproduces slowly—it can't be grown fast enough to make it cost effective. Shireen wondered if she could find a way—like plant tissue culture—to increase the stevia supply.

Methods and Results: Shireen experimented with different plant parts (called explants) and growth medium (including the addition of different kinds of sugars to boost development) over a period of 12 to 14 weeks. Starting from a single node, she was able to raise more than 75 plants! Shoot tips produced the most plants, and glucose provided the best help with shoot regeneration. Shireen's next step? She wants to survey diabetics and people on weight loss programs to see how well stevia works for them.

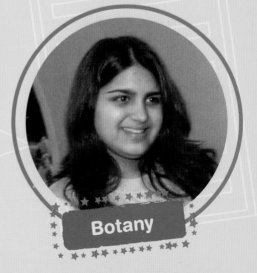

Botany

Nature vs. Nature:
Eradicating *Arundo donax* with
Allelopathic Leaf Extract Treatments
Susan Pasternak
Santa Barbara, California
Winner: Science Camp Award, 2005

Background: The fast-growing giant cane plant *Arundo donax* is used in the Southwest United States as an ornamental plant and to control erosion. In some areas, it has become so common that it is choking out other plants and clogging storm drains. Despite costing up to $15,000 an acre, the herbicide commonly used to destroy the giant cane only kills about 75 percent of the plants. Susan wanted to see if she could find a natural, more effective method of controlling the giant cane plant.

Methods and Results: In her search for a natural way to kill off *Arundo donax*, Susan decided to use allelopathic plants. These types of plants emit chemicals that can stop or limit the growth of other plants. She chose four different allelopathic plants and made extracts of them by boiling them in water. Then she applied the extracts to her test patch of giant cane plants. The extract of *Nerium oleander*, an evergreen shrub that grows in warm climates, proved the most effective, eliminating 98.5 percent of the giant cane plants.

Botany

For the Love of Lilies:
Finding a Cure for a Flower Fungus
Kyle Yawn
Bonaire, Georgia
Finalist, 2004

Background: There's a new plant fungus in town, and Kyle Yawn is fixing to take it out. Commonly known as daylily rust, it's so new to the United States that there's hardly any research on it—and certainly no cure. Kyle knew that the element silicon strengthened plant cell walls—the part of the plant the fungus attacked. Might a simple silicon solution cure the fungus among us? he wondered.

Methods and Results: With a donation of 100 or so infected plants from a local farmer, Kyle got down to work. He planted half in an experimental plot and watered the plants every day with a solution of silicon. The other half was planted in a control plot that got plain water. After two months, Kyle noted that the treated plants had fewer than one rust pustule per plant. An added benefit: The cure is environmentally safe. Since word of Kyle's success has gotten out, daylily enthusiasts have been calling him for advice. And he met with Dr. Jean Woodward—a plant pathologist at the University of Georgia and an expert on this fungus—to discuss his findings.

Botany

Botany

Watching the Grass Grow: The Effects of Reverse Osmosis Brine on Turfgrass
Christine Johns
Cape Coral, Florida
Finalist, 2004

Background: Many conservation-minded Floridians are helping the environment. One way is by using reclaimed wastewater to water their lawns and gardens. Christine Johns thought she could do better. What if she could use reverse osmosis brine, a byproduct of the water purification process that normally gets thrown away? Her hometown spends $200,000 a year to dispose of it!

Methods and Results: Christine decided to test the effects of the brine. She used it to water a new turfgrass called seashore paspalum. The turfgrass thrived! Not only that, but none of the potentially harmful metals present in the brine collected in the ground where the turfgrass was planted, according to Christine's tests. She concluded that the grass may act as a sponge to absorb the impurities. So using the brine preserves the water supply and it saves the community money—all in an environmentally friendly way.

More than Just Hot Air: Biogas Production from Bovine Excrement
Kevin Lane
Flora Vista, New Mexico
Finalist, 2004

Background: After reading about Oregon farmers who were producing usable biogas from domestic animal manure (that's right, cow poop!) to make electricity, Kevin's interest was sparked. He decided to see how much gas he could produce using equipment called an anaerobic digester (a sort of vacuum with heat) that was filled with cow manure and distilled water. He also wanted to see if he could increase the quantity generated by regularly depressurizing the digesters.

Methods and Results: After collecting and measuring out manure samples, Kevin placed the material in the digesters along with distilled water and turned the heat up to 98°F. He tested three different groups of specimens—one group was depressurized weekly, one group was depressurized biweekly, and one group was not depressurized. He measured the volume of the resulting gas and had a local laboratory analyze the samples for quality as measured in heat units (BTUs). The results: Depressurizing did help to produce more gas, but the biweekly schedule (fewer depressurizations) resulted in better quality gas. And that's not just hot air!

Chemistry

Chemistry

A Berry Good Pesticide: How Mistletoe Extract Compares to Commercial Pesticides
Adam Tazi
Orlando, Florida
Finalist, 2004

Background: Adam Tazi had already learned that you can make a natural pesticide from the unripe berries of the mistletoe plant. He wondered how his home brew would stack up against commercial chemicals like malathion and permethrin. He figured the chemicals might work better, but that the mistletoe extract would be safer for the environment.

Methods and Results: Adam mixed up pesticide and extract solutions of varying strengths. He placed 20 mosquito larvae in each solution and observed them all for three days. He also wanted to observe the pesticide solutions' effects on wildlife, so he made 3 percent solutions of all three and added three shrimp to each. His results were better than expected. The 3 percent mistletoe extract killed 95 percent of the mosquito larvae, but none of the shrimp! Compare this to the 3 percent chemical solutions, which were only about 50 percent effective on the larvae—and killed off all the shrimp. And the 5 percent malathion solution was enough to melt a plastic cup in one hour! Adam admitted that the chemicals may kill off adult mosquitoes, but that's just a small part of the problem. The population quickly rebounds because of the creatures' short life spans. His conclusion? Mistletoe is the smarter solution.

The Unbeatable Fire Ant: Do Commercial Fire Ant Traps Work?
Blake Thompson
Gainesville, Florida
Winner: Second Place, 2004

Background: As people who live down south know, fire ants are terrible pests! Blake Thompson's parents have tried any number of organic and alternative pesticides—soap, citrus oils, you name it—but without luck. Blake wondered: Would commercial bait traps work any better?

Methods and Results: First, Blake counted the ants to get a baseline population. He measured off three fields and placed index cards coated with peanut butter near the ant mounds in each field. After collecting the ant-filled cards, he froze them in order to safely count the individuals. Next, he designated one of the fields to be the control (no pesticide used) and set up two different kinds of commercial bait traps in the remaining fields. Each week, he repeated his population counts. Interestingly, he discovered that the pesticides only temporarily reduced the ant populations. The nests would empty when the traps were used, but new mounds shortly appeared nearby. And soon, the populations were back to their original counts.

Chemistry

Chemistry

Solar Production of Hydrogen from Seawater via Electrolysis
Nilesh Tripuraneni
Fresno, California
Winner: Second Place, 2005

Background: Nilesh became interested in environmentally friendly fuels and researched them to develop his science project. In his research, he learned about hydrogen-powered cars but found that traditional methods of producing hydrogen require fossil fuels. Nilesh decided to work on a more environmentally friendly way to produce hydrogen by using solar power.

Methods and Results: Nilesh designed and built a solar-powered device that ran an electrical current through a beaker full of saltwater. Through a process called electrolysis, the electrical current split the water into hydrogen and oxygen. Nilesh then measured the temperature, pressure, and volume of hydrogen produced. His findings indicate that hydrogen produced from seawater with solar-powered electrolysis is a promising alternative to fossil fuels.

Hidden Ethyl Alcohol in Soda Pop, Flavored Beverages, and Other Food Items
Gregory Lavins
Solon, Ohio
Winner: Image Maker Award, 2005

Background: Gregory read that bottled sparkling water sometimes contains small amounts of ethyl alcohol. He wondered if other bottled beverages also contained ethyl alcohol, since his research showed that drink manufacturers often use it during processing.

Methods and Results: Gregory selected 45 packaged beverages and tested each one in a measuring device called a gas chromatograph. This machine recorded the presence of any ethyl alcohol. Gregory found trace amounts of ethyl alcohol in almost all the beverages, with an average amount of .0238 percent of ethyl alcohol weight by volume. The highest concentration of ethyl alcohol in a beverage was .21 percent. Gregory then did a follow-up literature search on the safety of .21 percent ethyl alcohol in a beverage. His research convinced Gregory that this amount of ethyl alcohol would not harm people.

Chemistry

Earth Science

Shake Down:
The Effects of Liquefaction on Desert Soils
Eric Strege
La Quinta, California
Finalist, 2004

Background: For people who live in California, earthquakes are a part of life. Budding geologist Eric Strege was aware that many California cities are built on sandy desert soils. He wondered what happens to those soils in an earthquake. It turns out that desert soils shaken up by an earthquake behave a lot like liquids. The more they do so—or the higher the liquefaction rate—the greater the sink rate. What type of soil would remain most stable in an earthquake?

Methods and Results: Eric collected soil samples from ten different sites for testing. First, he used a purchased kit to determine the percentage of sand, silt, and clay in each. Then he built a frame with a concrete vibrator attached. Since the presence of groundwater is an important factor, Eric soaked his samples with water. Then he placed a wooden block on the surface and turned on the vibrator to shake up each sample. Eric measured how far the block sank—the farther it sank, the less stable the sample. He concluded that dense soils, which are not as susceptible to sudden pressure from rising groundwater, are the most stable. Eric hopes to do more work to find out how to make soil more stable and safer in earthquake-prone areas.

The Changing Ocean:
Population and Water Quality
Anastasia Roda
Lancaster, Pennsylvania
Finalist, 2004

Background: The population near Barnegat Bay, an estuary on the New Jersey coast, has quadrupled in the last 40 years. Anastasia Roda wondered if that kind of growth was having an adverse effect on the water quality of the bay.

Methods and Results: Originally, Anastasia planned to observe the water quality during the summer months only. The area is a big summer destination for many in the Northeast, and the population increases then. But a quick conversation with a local scientist convinced her to take a longer view, since it can take many years for water quality changes to become noticeable. Armed with more than 30,000 historical entries plus two months worth of data from her own twice-weekly tests at two different locations in the bay, Anastasia computed averages for each decade. Her suspicions were right on target! Four indicators of human impact on water quality showed a decline, especially the indicator on dissolved oxygen. Anastasia went a step further: She got a grant from the United States Environmental Protection Agency's National Estuary Program to create a pamphlet informing the public about the bay and how to protect it.

Earth Science

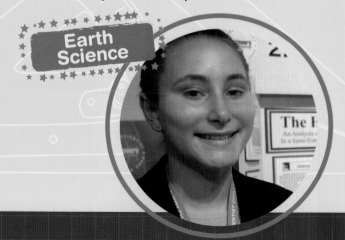

Mission: Rollover Reduction
Reducing Rollovers in 15-Passenger Vans
Nicholas Ekladyous
Imlay City, Michigan
Finalist, 2004

Background: Talk about great communicators! Nicholas Ekladyous certainly fits that description. Inspired by headlines regarding a fatal rollover crash involving a 15-passenger van, Nicholas started digging around. He discovered that because 15-passenger vans started out as cargo vans, they weren't subject to the same safety standards as normal passenger vehicles. These vans roll over more than any other van of their type, says the government. And the public doesn't even know!

Methods and Results: Nicholas and his uncle built a working scale model with which to experiment. Nicholas discovered that with the simple addition of an extra set of rear wheels, rollover stability could be increased to the equivalent of a subcompact car. That's a huge improvement! Next, Nicholas set out to inform the public. He shared his findings with automotive researchers via a teleconference with a consumer action group, created a Web site to summarize his report and conclusions, and continues to give personal presentations. "Educating the public," he says, "was my favorite part of the project."

Engineering

Paddle Perfection?
Seeking New Designs with Flume Testing
Mary Lou Hedberg
North Attleboro, Massachusetts
Winner: Third Place, 2005

Background: An avid kayaker, Mary Lou noticed the swirling waves made by her paddle. Did they represent wasted energy? If yes, was there a way her flat paddle could be made more efficient?

Methods and Results: Mary Lou devised a test to find the answers to her questions. First, she built her own flume (a testing device designed to supply a constant flow of water). Next, she analyzed her paddle stroke and learned that it involved both horizontal and vertical forces. Then she softened and reshaped plastic spoons to make model paddles and set up the flume to measure the forces on each paddle. After testing many different blades and shaft angles, Mary Lou found that a bent shaft and a hinged, spoon-shaped blade made the most efficient paddle. Mary Lou has now filed an application for a patent on her new design.

Engineering

75

Use It or Lose It:
Building a Solar Water Heater from an Automobile Radiator
Garrett Yazzie
Pinon, Arizona
Winner: Space Camp Award, 2005

Background: In Garrett's remote Navajo community, few people have electricity. For heat, they cut trees for firewood or haul coal from long distances. Garrett wanted to develop ways of harnessing and using solar energy to help his community. He decided to design and build a solar heater from an automobile radiator.

Methods and Results: Garrett built a solar heater with the radiator of a l967 Pontiac and 64 aluminum cans painted black. He designed the heater to provide hot air and hot water. He then measured the increases in air temperature and water temperature caused by the heater. In just one hour, the water temperature increased from 68°F to 201.2°F, close to the boiling point. In only 30 minutes, the air temperature from the heater reached 154.4°F. Garrett plans to use his invention to heat water for his mother and warm a room in their house during cold weather.

Blowin' in the Wind
Jacob Perry
Livingston, Montana
Finalist, 2005

Background: Because his state has a lot of wind power available as an energy source, Jacob became interested in wind turbines (machines that use wind power to produce electricity). He hypothesized that using longer blades would turn a turbine faster and thus produce more electricity.

Methods and Results: First, Jacob built his own wind turbine. As the blades of his turbine spun faster, they produced more electricity. Next, Jacob tested three blade lengths at three wind intensities (as simulated by three speeds of a hair dryer). Jacob found that the shortest blades performed best at high wind intensity, while the medium blades performed best at lower wind intensity. The longest blades actually performed the worst. Jacob thinks that the larger blades' higher wind resistance may be the reason they performed poorly.

Engineering

Engineering

Environmental Science

Plastics with a Purpose: Biodegradable Polymers and Their Composites
Pinaki Bose
Fort Worth, Texas
Finalist, 2005

Background: Just about everyone knows how much harm plastic refuse can cause sea creatures like seals and dolphins. If everyone knows this, wondered Pinaki Bose, why don't they make plastic polymers that degrade without creating harmful byproducts? The answer is, they do, but they cost too much to be commercially useful. Pinaki's next thought: Can a cheap, plentiful waste product like sawdust be used to create a cost-effective composite that might replace conventional plastics?

Methods and Results: After identifying a suitable biodegradable plastic polymer, Pinaki had to figure out a good material to replace some of it in order to reduce the cost. Sawdust was his material of choice— it was a readily available and cheap waste product (so he'd be recycling, too). He mixed fine sawdust with the heated polymer and tried out different forming techniques. Then he tested the resulting plastics for biodegradability, strength, and recyclability (in other words, could it be reused somehow). So far, Pinaki's study shows that he is on the right track: Adding sawdust can improve a polymer. His composites were recyclable and biodegradable, and one formula produced a stronger plastic than the unreinforced polymer.

An Analysis of Lead and Arsenic Contamination Levels in Butterfield Creek and Herriman
Spencer Larson
Springville, Utah
Winner: Team Award, 2005

Background: In his preliminary research, Spencer read an Environmental Protection Agency (EPA) report on possible lead and arsenic contamination in his area of Utah. He decided to research local environmental toxins. Spencer knew that around the turn of the 20th century, residue from nearby mines had been dumped into Butterfield Creek. The water picked up toxins from the mining residue and deposited them in the area of Herriman, near Spencer's hometown. Spencer hypothesized that he would find unacceptably high concentrations of lead and arsenic in the Herriman's soil and on the banks of Butterfield Creek.

Methods and Results: Spencer first collected soil samples from locations in his test area. He then dried and analyzed the samples using an advanced analysis technique called inductively coupled plasma testing. Many of Spencer's samples showed lead and arsenic levels above the national EPA standards.

Environmental Science

77

Environmental Science

Making Biodiesel Fuel from Soybean Oil
Colleen Ryan
Chillicothe, Ohio
Winner: Team Award, 2005

Background: After learning about the environmental problems caused by burning large amounts of fossil fuels, Colleen wanted to investigate an alternative fuel that was better for the environment. She decided to experiment with soybean-based fuel, because it is biodegradable. Also, the carbon dioxide released from burning soybean-based fuel is almost the same mass of carbon dioxide as the amount needed to grow the soybeans, so the fuel does not add significant carbon dioxide to the environment.

Methods and Results: First, Colleen made three liters of soybean fuel by combining soybean oil, ethanol, and a little sodium hydroxide. After letting the mixture settle, she separated soybean fuel from it by a process called decanting. She then measured the performance of her soybean fuel, using it to drive a new Ford truck on a closed course. When she compared the performance of the soybean fuel to a conventional diesel fuel, the conventional fuel had a 9 percent greater efficiency. However, Colleen also found that soybean biodiesel fuel could be mass produced more cheaply than petroleum-based diesel fuel and would cost about $1.25 per gallon.

Getting a Lead on Lead:
Lead Levels in Invertebrates Near
Herculaneum, Missouri
David Westrich
Cape Girardeau, Missouri
Winner: Third Place and Team Award, 2004

Background: David Westrich is a keen scientific observer. While performing an earlier experiment, he had noticed that lettuce leaves showed an increase in lead levels when the plants were exposed to soil contaminated with the heavy metal. He thought it would be logical to assume that creatures living close to a local smelter would show a similar increase.

Methods and Results: With the help of global positioning coordinates, David identified sites of varying distances from the smelter in nearby Herculaneum. Then he collected earthworm and woodlice specimens from each site. He dried and processed the specimens. Then he analyzed their remains for lead content using an instrument called a spectroscope. Bingo! His theory that lead levels would increase in creatures collected closer to the plant was absolutely correct.

Environmental Science

Mathematics

Tsunami Math:
Crunching the Numbers on Methane Hydrate
Kasey Borchardt
Vernon, Texas
Finalist, 2004

Background: Living in oil- and gas-rich Texas, Kasey Borchardt knows a bit about energy alternatives like gaseous hydrocarbon methane hydrate. The problem is that much of it lies buried in layers of sediment in the ocean floor. The natural release of the gas can cause underwater landslides. What would happen in a major explosion due to harvesting? Kasey asked herself. Could it be a tsunami in the making?

Methods and Results: Kasey did the math. First she created her own test in nearby swimming pools for confirmation and to help her calculate the speed of the resulting waves. Then she calculated how fast a tsunami originating along Blake Ridge (site of a large methane hydrate deposit off the coast of South Carolina) would travel. Her conclusions: A tsunami could hit the east coast of the United States in just over half an hour! That's too fast for people to evacuate. Kasey decided to share her results with those in charge. She even wrote to Tom Ridge, then chief of Homeland Security. So, what will happen when the United States ramps up its efforts to develop methane hydrate as an energy source? Kasey, calculator in hand, will be watching.

In a Heartbeat:
The Effects of Cell Phones on Pacemaker
Patients' Hearts
Joseph Stunzi
Watkinsville, Georgia
Winner: First Place, 2003

Background: Joseph's mother has worn a pacemaker, an electrical device that helps to regulate the beating of her heart, for several years. When Joseph's father, who works in the cell phone industry, started testing phones at home, Mrs. Stunzi complained about her heart rate increasing. What's up with that? Joseph wondered. Might the cell phones be causing the increase? Joseph was betting they did.

Methods and Results: Joseph got help from workers at a local heart center to put his experiment to the test. After recruiting pacemaker patients to be a part of his study, Joseph positioned them identically. Then he turned on an analog cell phone and held it three inches from the heart. He repeated the process with a digital cell phone. A pacemaker technician helped by taking an electrocardiogram, a test that measures heart rate, after each exposure. Joseph was right. Digital phones caused the most increase in heart rate. He also learned that pacemakers implanted after 2000 were less affected overall.

Medicine

Medicine

The Truth and Lies of Blood Glucose Monitoring Systems
Ruslan Werntz
Coppell, Texas
Winner: Science of Production Award, 2005

Background: Ruslan's father has Type 1 diabetes and needs to test the level of his blood sugar with a glucometer. At the doctor's, they were told that home-use glucometers are often less accurate than the glucometers used by physicians. That gave Ruslan the idea to test different home-use brands against a scientific glucometer called a Cardio-Chek, which is used in clinics, labs, and hospitals.

Methods and Results: Ruslan purchased five different brands of home-use glucometers. He then tested the glucose level of each human subject three times over two days with the home-use glucometers and the Cardio-Chek glucometer. In 120 tests, 79 of the home-use machines were at least 20 units off the results from the scientifically calibrated Cardio-Chek machine. Ruslan would like to make this information more widely available so diabetics will know that they need to check their home-use glucometers regularly against their doctor's more accurate machine.

The Little Engine That Could: Enhancing Traction Through Friction
Shannon McClintock
San Diego, California
Winner: First Place, 2004

Background: Shannon McClintock's grandfather, who used to work on the railroad, liked to tell Shannon about his work. He explained about using sand to help train cars gain traction on the rail lines. Might other materials work better? Shannon decided to find out.

Methods and Results: Shannon built a testing device with two flywheels touching each other. She then poured different materials—grits of sand, garnet, and slag—onto the spinning wheels. The results? Garnet grit outperformed the sand by 7 percent in adding traction! But the lower cost of sand, Shannon concluded, means it remains the grit of choice.

Physics

Physics

Sounds Good!
High Density Materials and Sound Reflection
Phillip Mansour
San Ramon, California
Finalist, 2004

Background: Phillip Mansour got interested in acoustics—the science of sound—in sixth grade. That's when he worked on a project about sound absorption. He wondered whether high-density materials would reflect more sound than low-density materials. In the seventh grade, he decided to find out more about it.

Methods and Results: Using special software and a computer with a speaker and a directional microphone, Phillip set to work. He tested 13 materials, including cork, wood, acrylic, glass, copper, and steel. He found that metals reflected sound better than non-metals, but density wasn't the only factor involved. If a material was dense and allowed for higher sound velocity through it, it tested better. So Phillip's hypothesis was partly correct, but it wasn't the whole story. In the meantime, Phillip is tuning in to possible applications for his research—ways to reduce noise pollution in an increasingly noisy world.

More Than Meets the Ear:
Making a Better Earplug
Celine Saucier
Midland, Michigan
Winner: Team Award, 2004

Background: Celine's parents were always telling her to wear earplugs when she mowed the lawn. Celine learned that hearing loss due to noise is temporary, but it can become permanent. Wearing earplugs works because the earplugs either block sound or absorb it. Celine thought she could do better. Why not make an earplug that does both?

Methods and Results: Sound is often a subjective matter, and Celine felt that the standard tests weren't strict enough. After devising her own stricter standards, Celine was in business. She tested rubber earplugs that block sound. She tested foam earplugs that absorb sound. And she tested two earplugs of her own design: One had foam plugs attached to the outer stems of rubber plugs, and one had metal and plastic caps attached to foam plugs. Both of Celine's designs beat the commercial plugs for noise reduction! In fact, Celine has applied for patents for her designs.

Physics

Physics

Will the Thermal Expansion of a Zinc Plate Undergoing the Photoelectric Effect Cause More Photoelectrons to Be Emitted?
Alexander Uribe
Eagle Mountain, Utah
Winner: Team Award, 2005

Background: Through his study of physics, Alexander became interested in the photoelectric effect (the ejection of electrons due to light). He decided to experiment with it in his project.

Methods and Results: Alexander built a test device that heated a zinc plate. He mounted the device on an electroscope, which would measure the number of photoelectrons emitted from the plate. Next, Alexander gave the plate an electrical charge by rubbing silk against a plastic pipe and rubbing the pipe against the zinc plate. He then heated the plate to different temperatures. Each time, he recorded how long it took the electroscope to read zero—that is, how long it took for the photoelectrons to be fully emitted (or discharged) from the plate. As he hypothesized, the heated plate discharged photoelectrons much faster than a cool plate. Alexander believes that the relationship he discovered could have several useful applications. For example, it could be used to make solar cells more efficient, to help make spacecraft more lightweight, and in ionizing air to make it cleaner and healthier for people to breathe.

Reduction of Drift in Model Rocketry
Anudeep Gosal
Orlando, Florida
Winner: Stargazer Award and Team Award, 2005

Background: Anudeep's hobby is building and launching model rockets. On windy days, his rockets sometimes drift away and get lost. Anudeep therefore decided to experiment with model rockets to find ways of reducing drift.

Methods and Results: Anudeep assembled and tested four groups of model rockets: 1) unmodified rockets that he launched vertically (his control group), 2) unmodified rockets that he launched at various angles, 3) rockets modified with fins tilted at 7 degrees, and 4) rockets with 7 grams of weight added to the nose cone. He then launched each group of rockets ten times, measuring the distance from launch to touchdown. (He had previously built homemade measuring tools for this task.) Anudeep found that his control group (unmodified rockets launched vertically) averaged 99 feet of drift, while each of the other groups drifted less. In the future, Anudeep hopes that he and other model rocketeers can save time and money by using his design ideas to reduce drift in their rockets.

Space Science

Zoology

A Spectral Analysis of the Effects of Light Pollution on the Pennsylvania Firefly
Brendan Dwyer
Northport, New York
Finalist, 2005

Background: In his research on fireflies, Brendan found that some scientists are worried that light pollution may interfere with firefly mating. Fireflies flash their lights to find mates, and too much artificial light may confuse them.

Methods and Results: Brendan has been studying fireflies for three years and had already measured the strongest light in which they could signal. This year, he began analyzing the wavelengths produced by typical urban lights and by fireflies. He found that fireflies could signal even in bright light and that they could respond to a wide range of light wavelengths. Only one source of urban light, high-pressure sodium bulbs, appeared to interfere with the fireflies' communications.

Asian Invaders (Banded Elm Bark Beetles): Are They Lurking in Your Town?
Bailey Terry
Newcastle, Wyoming
Finalist, 2005

Background: Bailey's father, a state forester, told her about a species of beetle called banded elm bark invaders. These beetles are often found in shipping crates, but not much else is known about them. Bailey did preliminary research and found that elm trees are the only type of tree on which the beetles have been found in the United States. She decided to study the beetle's life cycle to learn more about it.

Methods and Results: Bailey started by studying a Siberian elm infested with the beetles. She observed that the beetles' life cycle was about one month. During the beetles' life cycle, Bailey observed fine sawdust where the beetles bored into the tree. Later, she saw the beetle larvae feeding on the cambium layer of the tree and turning the cambium to mush. Next, Bailey observed the beetles on samples from an American elm tree and other local tree species. She found that the beetles died off in each tree sample except the two types of elm tree she observed. Bailey concluded that the elms are in the most danger from this type of beetle.

Zoology

Science Project Handbook

So you want to do a great science project! Here's a step-by-step guide to help you do your best work.

1 Getting Started: Choose a Topic

When you're thinking about a topic, start with things that interest you. You'll be working on your project for at least two or three months, and you don't want to get bored. If you're curious about your topic, the project will be more fun. Also, you'll be more likely to do a good job. Don't pick a hard subject just because you think it will impress the judges. If the topic is too hard, you may get discouraged and want to quit—or you may not know the answers when the judges ask you questions.

Need an Idea?

Some **DCYSC** winners have gotten ideas for great projects from hobbies or family activities. Anudeep Gosal got a project idea from his hobby. As a member of his school's rocket club, Anudeep enjoyed launching model rockets. But he hated it when his rockets got caught by the wind and drifted off course or fell in a nearby lake. For his winning project, Anudeep decided to design and test rockets that would be less likely to drift away.

Finalist Kelsey Burnham's father spurred her interest in the effect of silicon on plant growth in South Florida soils. He returned home from an agricultural meeting excited about a new soil additive designed to help plant growth. She put the soluble silicon additive to the test to discover whether or not it really worked.

Colleen Ryan was worried about the environmental effects of petroleum and other fossil fuels, so she researched alternatives. When she learned about soybean-based bio-diesel, the fact that it is biodegradable made it seem ideal. She produced 3 liters and compared it with conventional fuel in a truck on a 3-mile course. Even though conventional fuel offered more miles per gallon, Colleen discovered that her soy-based bio-diesel can be mass produced at a lower cost than conventional fuel and sold for about $1.25 per gallon.

Ruslan Werntz's father has Type 1 diabetes. To stay healthy, he has to test his blood glucose level regularly to make sure he's eating the right balance of foods. When his father's doctor ran a glucometer test whose result was 30 points lower than his father's home test just a short time earlier, Ruslan was surprised. The doctor said home-use glucometers weren't as accurate as the more expensive tools doctors use, so Ruslan set out to confirm the doctor's statement.

2 Research Your Topic

Once you have a topic in mind, you're ready to do research. Look for books and magazines on your subject at the library or local bookstore. The Internet is a great way to do research, but some Internet resources are more reliable than others. It's a good idea to find out who wrote the Web site you're using as a reference so you can be sure it's one you can trust to have accurate information. When you read different sources of information, take careful notes, including where you got the information. Then you can list the sources in the bibliography of your project report. If you need help, ask your teacher or a librarian how best to document the sources you use.

Once you have done some background reading on your topic, you may also want to do primary research—the kind of research you do on your own. You could write or talk to people who know about your topic or do some preliminary experiments.

3 Make a Detailed Plan

After researching your topic, make a detailed plan of your project based on the scientific method. The scientific method is a series of techniques or steps for your project that are designed to help you observe, investigate, and test the hypothesis or question you want to answer. Your plan should include the question or problem you want to solve, what you think your project will prove, and the materials and methods you'll use to construct your experiment or test. Be sure that your plan also covers what you'll actually do during the experiment, what the results mean (your analysis of the data you collect), and your conclusions—what you learned from the experiment.

A Good Plan Includes the Following:

Purpose of Your Project: Why are you doing your experiment? What things do you want to find out? What is the problem you want to solve?

Experimental Question or Hypothesis: A hypothesis is a prediction of what you think the outcome of your project will be. (For example, you might predict that plants grown with fertilizer will grow faster than plants grown without fertilizer. That prediction is the hypothesis of your experiment.)

Materials and Methods: For this part of your plan, list any supplies or materials you will need. Then write down a detailed description of the methods you will use to do your experiment. Will you need to work in a lab? What will you change during the experiment to test your hypothesis?

Be very specific when you describe the way you'll construct your experiment. Don't forget to include information about the variables you plan to use. Variables are factors that you change or evaluate in order to test your hypothesis. Experimental or independent (manipulated) variables are the things you change on purpose to test your hypothesis.

Dependent (responding) variables are the changes that occur in response to the experimental variable. Controls are the things that must remain the same every time you conduct your experiment.

The only part of your experiment that you can alter is the independent variable. For example, if you're testing different concentrations of fertilizer on plants, you can't also change the amount of light the plants get. You can only change your independent or experimental variable. Plan to repeat your test or experiment several times. By repeating the experiment under the same conditions, you'll be able to evaluate and compare the results you get each time you conduct the test.

Project Schedule: It's also good to plan a detailed schedule for your work—and to allow plenty of time. Most science projects take a minimum of eight weeks from start to presentation, so plan on allowing at least that much time. (Some of the **DCYSC** winners worked on their projects for over a year!)

Allow Yourself Extra Time

Your experiment may take longer than you expect, so it's smart to schedule extra time for it. When her whole plant experiment got contaminated in the lab, Neela Thangada had to throw out 60 plant cultures and start over. Luckily, she had begun her project early and had plenty of time to perform her experiment over again from the beginning. This time, she got great results. She even went on to win top **DCYSC** honors in the Forces of Nature challenge!

4 Conduct the Experiment

Now you're ready to begin your experiment, following the plan that you have written. While you work, be sure to keep detailed notes on everything you do and observe. Scientists make notes on just about everything during an experiment, so follow their example. Write down dates, times, descriptions of good results, or even messed-up results. You never know what might be important later! You also might want to make sketches of the things you observe or take photographs of your work. In order to accurately analyze your results, the data you collect must also be accurate. All these records will help you write your report and make a display.

Note This

Here's what **DCYSC** prize-winner Colleen Ryan learned about note-taking during her project: "At first, my notebook was just a pad that I jotted things down on. I was surprised to discover that every single adult I spoke with asked to see my notebook. I finally had to learn to keep my notes properly." Colleen believes that keeping careful, detailed notes helped make her project a winner.

5 Analyze Your Results

When you finish your experiment, take time to organize your notes. You may even want to recopy or type some of the notes so they are more organized and easier to follow. It might help to take your raw data (the information you collected when you did your project) and make a table, chart, or graph so that you can look at your results from a different point of view.

Tables, charts, and graphs are diagrams that show the relationship between numbers visually. They use math to provide a clear picture and arrange the results in a way that an observer can understand quickly. Sometimes they show you things that would be hard to see otherwise. (Computer programs such as Excel can help you make graphs from your data.)

Compare your data so that you can analyze the meaning of your results. Ask yourself what happened in the experiment, if the results you got agree with your hypothesis or not, what (if any) problems occurred, and so forth. Sometimes scientists get results they didn't expect, for example, results that don't agree with their hypothesis. This could happen to you. If it did and you have time, you may want to repeat the experiment again to see if you come up with the same unanticipated results. Many times, scientists' hypotheses aren't supported by the results of their experiments.

Whether or not your hypothesis is supported by your experiment, you must report the truth in your conclusion. If your research supported your hypothesis, you should state that in your report. If you expected what happened, discuss that. If your research supported your hypothesis but your experimental results didn't, you must report that as well. Report everything. Say what you expected and what actually happened. If you think you know why the results didn't support your ideas and you believe you know the reason, offer the scientific explanation for the results you got. Then describe what you would do to change the project and improve upon it the next time.

Happy Accidents

Sometimes the unexpected results of research lead to an important discovery. Penicillin, the first antibiotic, was found by accident. (Antibiotics are substances released by bacteria that prevent the growth of other organisms without hurting the host.)

ALEXANDER FLEMING

PENICILLIUM NOTATUM

©RED

Alexander Fleming was researching antibacterial agents (substances that can slow or stop the growth of bacteria) while working at a London hospital in 1928. Before going off on vacation, he left several of his culture dishes (petri dishes) sitting out. On his return, Fleming found that the petri dishes were contaminated and piled them up in some disinfectant. When he retrieved a few that had not been submerged to show a visitor what he'd been working on, Fleming noticed something unusual. A petri dish he'd smeared with Staphylococcus bacteria was completely overgrown—except for a clear area surrounding a growth of mold. Spores of the mold, a rare type called *Penicillium notatum*, had apparently drifted into his lab from the room below where a mycologist (mold expert) was collecting molds for an asthma researcher.

Deducing that something in the mold was stopping the growth of the bacteria, Fleming grew more of the mold in a separate, pure culture. When he tested it, he found he was correct. The mold produced a substance that killed a variety of disease-causing bacteria. He named the substance penicillin after the mold it came from. Fleming's discovery led to further research, both by himself and other scientists, which eventually revealed that penicillin could in fact save lives and changed the way bacterial infections are treated.

6 Write the Report

Your written report is one of the most important parts of your project. A great report can make an average project look good, and a poor report can hurt a good project. So sharpen your pencil and work hard on your report—it will pay off! When you write your report, include the following sections:

Title Page: Note the title of your project, your name and address, your school, your grade, and the name of your science teacher.

Table of Contents: List the page number for the start of each section in your report.

Introduction: This section includes 1) some background information on your project (how you got your idea, etc.) and 2) your hypothesis or experimental question.

Experiment: Describe in detail the materials and methods you used to do your experiment and gather your data. Include enough detail that someone reading your report could actually perform your experiment.

Discussion: Explain the steps you took in reaching your conclusions. Compare your results to your hypothesis (what you predicted the data would show). Did your data uphold your hypothesis or did it show something different? Also, explain what you might do differently if you did the project again.

Conclusion: Summarize your results. Don't mention anything in this section that was not discussed earlier in your report.

Acknowledgments: List and thank the people who helped you. Also mention any institutions or businesses that provided assistance.

References: Your list of references should include any books, articles, or Internet resources that you used in your research. For the right format, see the rules for your science fair competition, check with your science or English teacher, or ask a librarian.

7 Make a Display

Your display is crucial to your success at a science fair. With a good display, you can show people exactly what your project is about and how you did it. Your display needs to be tidy and well organized, but it doesn't need flashing lights or other fancy gimmicks. When you make your display, be sure to include these sections: background information, the topic or problem, your prediction or hypothesis, your methods, your results and conclusion, your written report, and any graphs or charts you have made. If you took photos or made any drawings, it's a good idea to include them in your display.

8 Plan and Rehearse Your Presentation

You've finished your project and written your report. Now it's time to present your work. Plan what you're going to say in your oral presentation. You might even want to outline your speaking notes on index cards. Take time to rehearse your presentation, too. Start by rehearsing on your own. Once you are comfortable doing that, ask a friend or a family member to listen to your presentation. If you practice, you will be more relaxed and do a better job when you talk to the judges. Remember, you are judged partly on how well you communicate your ideas.

9 It's Show Time!

Now you're ready to roll. On the big day, dress neatly and comfortably. Your careful preparation will pay off because you'll know what you're talking about. If the judges do happen to ask you a question that you're not sure about, tell them that you're not sure but you would like to look into the question and learn the answer. Don't pretend you know an answer that you don't really know. Remember to look at the judges when they talk with you and feel proud of what you've accomplished. After all, you're an expert on your project.

How to Enter the DCYSC

The *Discovery Channel Young Scientist Challenge* **is the only national science competition of its kind for middle grade students. It was established in 1999 by Discovery Communications, Inc., and Science Service, a nonprofit organization founded in 1921 to "advance public understanding and appreciation of science among people of all ages." Nominees for the** DCYSC **have a chance to win a $20,000 scholarship and the title of America's Top Young Scientist of the Year.**

To become eligible for the **DCYSC**, you must 1) be in the fifth through eighth grade and 2) join the more than 60,000 middle grade students who compete in **DCYSC**-affiliated science fairs that take place around the country in the spring. Based on the quality of your science project and your ability to clearly communicate your knowledge and ideas, you may be one of the 6,000 entrants nominated by their fair directors to enter their projects in the **DCYSC**. If you are nominated, you'll receive a lapel pin, a certification of recognition, and an entry form for the national competition.

Between June and early September, the judges will pick 400 semifinalists from the 6,000 entrants. Once again you'll be judged on the scientific merit of your work and on your ability to communicate the science of your project. If you are chosen as a semifinalist, you'll receive a certificate of recognition, a small prize, and a chance to move on to the next stage.

To become one of the 40 finalists, your written and visual presentations must show that you understand your research by providing all the information in a logical, easily interpreted manner. You must demonstrate that you can explain your project and the underlying science and that you are comfortable discussing both your project and science in general. If you are chosen as a finalist, you'll receive several prizes, including a trip to Washington, D.C., where you'll present your science project to the judges and team up with four other finalists to compete with seven other teams in several theme-related challenges, such as Forces of Nature in 2005 and All About Physics in 2004, for various awards and prizes.

The top prize is a $20,000 scholarship and the title of America's Top Young Scientist of the Year. The second place winner will take home a $15,000 scholarship and the third place winner, a $7,500 scholarship. The other 36 finalists will each receive a $500 scholarship.

Can you imagine yourself standing on a podium with all the television cameras focused on you as you're presented with the first prize? Then what are you waiting for? Find a **DCYSC**-affiliated science fair, devise a terrific science project, and enter the competition!

The entry form has four parts:

1 Student, Project, and School Information

Among the information you'll include in this section are the name of your science fair; your name; personal and family information; the title and scientific category of your project, where you conducted your lab work and what it involved (for example, bacteria or plants); and information about your school.

2 Extracurricular Activities

In this section, you'll note what extracurricular activities you've been involved with; what hobbies or activities you enjoy and why; what career you're interested in pursuing and why; and what inspired your interest in science in general and your project in particular.

3 Essay Questions

This part requires you to write three essays (typed and double-spaced) that explain, evaluate, and communicate about your science fair project. You must also include a one-page visual aid (such as a diagram or chart) to help explain your project.

4 Certifications

Here is where you certify that all the information you've included is true and have a parent or guardian sign a certification and release agreement, allowing you to participate in the **DCYSC** and granting permission to Discovery Communications and Science Service to use your name and biographical information in advertising and promotion for the competition.

In order to be eligible, you must mail your completed entry form in time to reach Science Service by the deadline in June.

To find a DCYSC affiliated fair, go to:
http://www.sciserv.org/dcysc/Fairs/FAIRLIST.ASP
Select your state from the pull-down menu at the bottom of the page. The fairs are listed by city in alphabetical order.

GLOSSARY

acceleration   the rate of change of an object's speed and direction

accelerometer   an instrument for measuring acceleration

air pressure   the pressure, or force, exerted by the motion of molecules in the atmosphere

anemometer   an instrument for measuring wind speed

antibiotics   substances released by bacteria that prevent the growth of other organisms without harming the host

barometer   an instrument for measuring air pressure

barometric pressure   see air pressure

Bernoulli principle   a principle that states that the pressure in a fluid decreases the faster the fluid moves

biohazard   a biological product that poses a hazard to people or the environment

control   a factor that stays the same in an experiment and a standard of comparison for checking the experiment's results

drag   the resistance caused by an object as it moves through air

earthquake   a shaking of the ground usually caused by the release of stress along a fracture in the Earth's crust

frequency   the number of waves, such as sound or light, that crest in one second

gravity   the force of attraction between objects

hurricane   a large tropical storm with powerful, circular winds

hypothesis   a prediction about an experiment's outcome that can be tested

general theory of relativity   Albert Einstein's expansion of the special theory of relativity to include accelerated motion, which states that the effects of acceleration and gravity are equivalent and that acceleration and gravity warp (bend) light (An example of this can be seen in the bottom photo on page 30, which shows light from distant stars [visible as arcs] warped by a massive cluster of galaxies)

laser   a device producing a beam of high-energy light

lift   an upward force caused by streams of air passing around an aircraft's wing

MAV (micro aerial vehicle)   tiny aircraft operated through remote controls

microorganism   an organism that can only be seen through a microscope

molecule   a substance's smallest particle, made up from atoms

momentum   an object's mass multiplied by its velocity

Newton's third law of motion   For every action, there is an equal and opposite reaction

pendulum   a weight that swings back and forth on a string

photoelectric effect   the act of converting light into electricity

quantum physics   a branch of science that studies the physics of the atom

Richter scale   a scale used to measure the intensity of earthquakes

special theory of relativity   Albert Einstein's 1905 theory of space and time, which states that the laws of nature are all the same in uniformly moving frames of reference and that the speed of light in open space never varies regardless of the frame of reference; this theory replaces Newtonian mechanics at very high velocities

supercell   a severe thunderstorm with deep, rotating winds; many develop into tornadoes

tectonic plate   a large piece of the Earth's crust

thrust   the force that propels an airplane or rocket through the air

tornado   a rotating column of air that moves at high speeds and is capable of causing destruction

tsunami   large ocean waves caused by earthquakes, volcanic eruptions, landslides, explosions, or meteor impacts

vaporize   to convert or be converted into vapor

variable   a factor that can change and affect an experiment's result

velocity   the speed and direction of an object

vibration   a rapidly repeated back-and-forth movement

volcano   an opening in the Earth that ejects lava, gases, and ash

vortex   a whirling mass of air or water

wind shear   a change in wind direction and speed

wind tunnel   a device used to study the effects of wind flow

wing warping   a system for controlling the flight of an aircraft by raising and lowering its wing tips